THE OFFICIAL

Liverpool

FANS' GUIDE

THIS IS A CARLTON BOOK

This edition published in 1997

10 9 8 7 6 5 4 3 2 1

A CIP catalogue record for this book is available from the British Library

ISBN 1 85868 326 2

Project Editor: Martin Corteel
Project art direction: Paul Messam
Production: Garry Lewis and Sarah Schuman
Picture research: Victoria Walker
Designed by Jim Stanton

Author's acknowledgements
With thanks to everyone who has made this book possible; particularly
the players who made and recounted the club's history, the *Liverpool
Echo* for providing much source material, Martin Corteel at Carlton
Books for editing the manuscript, mum and dad, and my neglected wife
Lucy for all her help, support and life-saving supply of chocolate biscuits.

Selected bibliography
Walmsley, David: *Liverpool's Greatest Players*, The Official Guide
(Headline, 1996)
Pead, Brian: *Liverpool, A Complete Record* (Breedon Books, 1990)
Robinson, Michael (ed): *Liverpool FC, The 25 Year Record* (Soccer Book
Publishing, 1995)

Printed in Italy

THE OFFICIAL
Liverpool

YOU'LL NEVER WALK ALONE

LIVERPOOL
FOOTBALL CLUB

EST. 1892

FANS' GUIDE

THE STORY OF
THE PREMIER LEAGUE YEARS

DAVID WALMSLEY

CARLTON

Contents

Paul Ince is a new kid on the Anfield block

Manager Roy Evans has been boss since 1994

The Shankly Gates' message is plain and simple

*Looks at how a club that was founded in the
aftermath of a split from Everton FC in 1892
went on to become the most powerful side in
Europe during the 1970s and early '80s.*

*Examines Liverpool's fortunes in the five years
since the Premiership began – the excitement
and passion and the highs and lows.*

*Describes the domination of Europe by
Liverpool for a decade during the 1970s and
early 1980s, including comprehensive
coverage of all four European Cup triumphs.*

*Reviews the great tradition of Liverpool in
the domestic Cups, with full details of all 11
FA Cup Final appearances as well as the five
League Cup victories.*

Introduction

Liverpool Football Club emerged from humble beginnings, to grow in stature as the twentieth century progressed to become the greatest club in Europe during the late 1970s and early '80s. With the dawn of the Premiership in August 1992, Liverpool have entered a new era and now, with the likes of Robbie Fowler and Paul Ince thrilling the Anfield crowds, the Reds are set to reclaim their English footballing throne.

Liverpool are the greatest club in English football history, of that there can be no doubt. To those Manchester United fans who point to the success of their club in recent years, look at United's track record in Europe and then compare it to Liverpool's.

During the 1970s and early '80s, the Reds swept all before them in European competition, winning the European Cup four times, the UEFA Cup twice and finishing runners-up in the 1981 World Club Championship.

The catalyst for Liverpool's emergence was the appointment of Bill Shankly as manager in 1959. The Scot set about putting in place a tradition and a "Liverpool" way of doing things that is still maintained faithfully to this day.

After Shankly, came Bob Paisley and the winning habit continued throughout the late 1970s and into the '80s as the silverware kept Anfield's trophy cabinet full.

In the 1990s, the trophies may have dwindled, but Liverpool continue to represent everything that is good about the English game.

The Premiership title has yet to come to Liverpool, but the new generation of stars thrilling the Kop is every bit as exciting as the Roger Hunts and Kevin Keegans of the past.

With foreign names such as Patrik Berger and Karlheinz Riedle playing alongside Robbie Fowler and Paul Ince, Liverpool have some truly world-class stars in their side.

Every aspect of Liverpool FC. is dealt with in this book from their origins way back in 1892 to the development throughout this century including details of all 18 Championship wins.

But particular attention is given to the Liverpool of the 1990s – the Premiership Years – the star players, the new-look Anfield stadium, the great Premiership matches and complete statistics of all games. If you're a true Red, this book is for you.

German striker Karlheinz Riedle was one of Liverpool's signings over the summer of 1997

The History of Liverpool

Founded in 1892 after a dispute with Everton FC, Liverpool rose to become one of the leading clubs in England before achieving European domination in the '70s

In the Beginning

At the dawn of organised football in Britain there were no shortage of Nomads and Wanderers, clubs which began life without a home ground of their own. Liverpool FC, however, was born in entirely different circumstances: created to occupy a stadium that already existed.

For the first 13 years soccer in the city was dominated by just one club – Everton. And between 1884 and 1892 their home was in Anfield Road, on a patch of land owned by wealthy brewers John and Joseph Orrell. The club president was another brewer, John Houlding, and it wasn't long before he was also Everton's landlord. A long-running row over rent rises then ensued, coming to a head in 1892 when Houlding was voted out of the presidency, and a split became inevitable. Everton quit Anfield to move to Goodison Park on March 12. They kept the name, Houlding kept the ground and three days later founded the Liverpool Football Club and Athletic Grounds Company Limited. The story of the Reds had begun.

Liverpool's application to join the new second divi-sion of the Football League was rejected, but they gained entry the following year after winning the Lancashire League and Liverpool District Cup in their very first season. They started their league career as they intended to continue, by storming straight to the top. Liverpool were unbeaten throughout 1893–94 to take the second-division title and gain promotion through a Test Match victory over Newton Heath. However, things did not continue as planned, and the Anfield side were relegated the following term.

They bounced back immediately, however, scoring 106 goals and remaining unbeaten at home on their way to the second division crown and another promotion via a play-off. This time they consolidated their position, reached the FA Cup semi-final in 1897 and '99, and in the latter year lost the Championship on the final day of the season. But the new century brought new fortune for Liverpool; and, guided by centre-half Alex Raisbeck and striker Sam Raybould, they took their first league title by going unbeaten in their final 12 games of the 1900–01 season.

That Championship joy was to be short-lived, for within three years Liverpool had again been relegated. But once more the Anfield men rebounded at the first attempt — and this time they went straight on to reclaim the Championship. Raisbeck and Raybould still remained from the club's last title-winning side, but in 1905—06 the signing of Chesterfield goalkeeper Sam Hardy and Sunderland striker Jack Hewitt made the difference.

Liverpool then yo-yoed up and down the top flight for the remainder of the pre-Great War years. The

Alex Raisbeck (1898–1909)

Scottish centre-half Alex Raisbeck was the first in a long and illustrious line of Anfield superstars. A strong, striking figure with distinctive fair hair and a walrus moustache, he was the driving force behind Liverpool's first two Championship successes, in 1900–01 and 1905–06.

Although standing only 5ft 9ins tall, he packed plenty of power into his frame and could outjump opponents much taller than him. Blessed with electric pace, he earned a reputation as one of the most stylish players of his day, captivating spectators and opponents alike with his surges forward from defence. After he inspired Scotland to an unexpected victory over England in Hampden Park's first international, played in 1906, visiting goalkeeper James Ashcroft declared: "I never saw such play. I could not keep my eyes off him."

Raisbeck won eight Scotland caps, but was as loyal to his club as he was to his country, turning down an international call in his first season to help Liverpool's ultimately vain pursuit of a League and Cup double. That was in 1899, after he had arrived at Anfield following spells at Hibernian and Stoke. Liverpool were sufficiently keen on the defender from Stirlingshire to pay him £4 a week, at a time when professionalism was the exception rather than the rule. In the 11 seasons that followed, during which time the club's successes were built on the rock of their Raisbeck-led defence, the cushing Scot proved himself worth every penny.

Born: Polmont, Stirlingshire, 1879
Height: 5 ft 9in
Weight: 12st 7lb
Position: Defender
Games: 340
Goals: 21
Previous clubs: Hibernian, Stoke City
Honours: League Championship 1900–01, 1905–06
International status: Scotland international

season after their title triumph, they needed a last-day win over their successors Newcastle to avoid the drop, but 12 months later finished as runners-up. In 1911–12 they again needed closing victories to preserve their first division status, but as the stormclouds of war began to gather over Europe, the Reds reached their first-ever FA Cup final, only to lose to Burnley by a solitary goal at the Crystal Palace.

The championship-winning Liverpool team of 1905–06 with Alex Raisbeck middle row, sixth from left

Between the Wars

ALTHOUGH the First World War ended in 1918, football in England did not resume in earnest until the following year. When it did, Liverpool wasted little time in re-establishing themselves among the game's elite, finishing fourth in the first two campaigns and only missing out on the title through a lack of firepower.

But then as the Roaring Twenties began things clicked for the Reds, and they picked up back-to-back Championships in 1921—22 and 1922—23. These teams, under the guidance of Dave Ashworth, were some of the finest in the club's history. Few of the pre-war heroes remained, but there was a whole new batch to take their place. With the incomparable Elisha Scott in goal, Liverpool's rearguard was further strengthened by the likes of the Rev. James "Parson" Jackson — a pacy full-back who went on to captain the club — Thomas "Tiny" Bradshaw, who combined the build of Ron Yeats with the touch of Alan Hansen, and hard men Jock McNab and Walter Wadsworth, the former of whom liked to warm up for a match with a couple of pints of Guinness.

Another defender, Donald McKinlay, was the captain of the double title-winning team and chipped in with some vital goals through the trademark power and accuracy of his free-kick repertoire. But the main attacking threat in that side came from the left-wing pairing of Harry Chambers and Fred Hopkin. Chambers, nicknamed "Smiler" by the fans and "Sharky" by his team-mates, looked an unlikely hero with his bow legs, toothless grin and pigeon-toes. But he was a prolific goalscorer who topped the Reds' scoring charts in each of the first five seasons after the First World War, and struck 41 times in the 72 matches of those Championship seasons. Hopkins was the provider in the partnership, and scored so rarely that there was much amusement when his first goal for the club coincided with the outbreak of a fire in one of the Anfield stands.

The Liverpool team were also on fire during those title years, taking the 1921—22 prize with a run of only two defeats in 31 games. The following term they racked up a record-equalling points total and the defence conceded just 31 goals in 42 matches, an all-time low that would only be broken by another

Liverpool pose for the cameras in 1922–23 having won their second consecutive Division One title

Anfield side almost half a century later.

But during the late '20s and early '30s the Reds slumped into mediocrity, managing no better than fourth place in the League and never threatening to end their FA Cup jinx. The arrival of South African Gordon Hodgson in 1925 provided a new source of goals to keep the team afloat, and in 1930—31 he hit a club record of 36 goals, including four hat-tricks. His final tally of 232 league goals remained unbeaten for 30 years. Though Hodgson was transferred to Leeds United in 1936, manager George Kay was beginning to build another outstanding Liverpool side — one which was sadly to be denied a chance to show its true greatness by another seven years of war.

Elisha Scott – small but perfectly formed

Elisha Scott (1912–34)

LIVERPOOL have employed many great goalkeepers over the years, but few have bettered the exploits of Ulsterman Elisha Scott. Initially turned down by several clubs for being too small at five feet nine, he was brought to Anfield at the age of 17 and went on to make more than 450 appearances in his 21 years at the club.

Slim and agile, Scott was one of the most popular of all Liverpool players — and one of the most colourful too. He wore knee-pads to protect himself from hard pitches and cold weather in winter, and would constantly bawl instructions to the defenders in front of him. But he inspired the teams in which he played by deed as well as by word, and his contribution was vital to the Championship successes of 1921—22 and 1922—23. He was just as heroic on the international scene, playing for Ireland until he was in his forties and steering them to a famous win over Scotland in 1928.

His brother Billy was keeping goal for Everton when Elisha signed for Anfield, but his most celebrated derby battles were with the Blues' record goalscorer, Dixie Dean. Legend has it that the pair once passed on opposite sides of Everton Valley and when Dean nodded a greeting, Scott automatically threw up his hands to make a save! Everton actually tried to sign the 'keeper in 1934 but were rebuffed after a wave of protest from Liverpool fans. They knew a gem when they saw one.

Born: Belfast, Ulster, 1894
Height: 5ft 9in
Position: Goalkeeper
Games: 467
Goals: None
Previous clubs: None
Honours: League Championship 1921-22, 1922-23
International status: Ireland international

From War to Revolution

ONCE again, Liverpool returned to peacetime football with a bang. And this time their wait for the Championship was the shortest possible, as the very first title of the post-war period belonged to Anfield.

The nucleus of the side had been put together before the outbreak of war, when Billy Liddell, Bob Paisley, Jack Balmer, Willie Fagan and Cyril Done all came into the first-team picture. At the end of hostilities, manager George Kay added the likes of Cyril Sidlow, Ray Lambert, Laurie Hughes, Bill Jones, Phil Taylor and Albert Stubbins. Stubbins was a £13,000 record signing from Newcastle United and only joined Liverpool because he had spoken to them first, after the Reds had won the opportunity by tossing a coin with Everton. But the Geordie went on to become a Liverpool legend and, with Balmer, scored the goals that won his new team the 1946—47 Championship.

With Sidlow reliable in goal, Taylor and Paisley providing skill and strength at wing-half, Laurie Hughes heading for England recognition at centre-back and the Stubbins-Balmer combination up-front, the title win was a triumph for teamwork. But if that side had one outstanding star, it was winger Billy Liddell, who illuminated every team in which he played with his artistry and determination. And Liverpool needed all that commitment to win one of the tightest-ever Championship finishes. With one round of matches still to play in a season extended into June by a string of winter postponements, four teams were in with a chance. Two of them — Wolverhampton Wanderers and Liverpool — met at Molineux, and the Reds came out on top through a superb Stubbins goal that clinched a 2—1 win. But they had to wait another fortnight to be assured of the title by Stoke City's defeat at Sheffield United, a result confirmed by an almighty roar from the Kop as their heroes beat Everton in the Liverpool Senior Cup final.

However, that team had spent its best years fighting the Second World War; and although the Reds reached the 1950 FA Cup final, losing 2—0 to Arsenal,

Another season, another title – The Liverpool Championship-winning side of 1946–47

they were already beginning to decline. George Kay was forced into retirement by ill-health and his successor Don Welsh proved unable to halt the slide. Kay's final two years saw Liverpool finish eighth and ninth before, under Welsh, falling to 11th, then 17th twice and finally 22nd in 1954. Liverpool had been relegated for only the third time in their history — and no one could say they didn't deserve it. They had lost a record 23 games and conceded a worst-ever 97 goals, a tally no other team in the entire League could match.

Previous experience suggested the Anfield men would bounce straight back at the first attempt, but this time their exile was to be a frustratingly lengthy one. However, at one point in their first season out of the top flight they looked like plummeting into the third division and suffered a record 9—1 defeat at Birmingham City. They conceded 96 goals, but 92 in their favour helped them scramble up to 11th place. Although winger Alan A'Court and goalkeeper

Tommy Younger were good enough to play for England and Scotland respectively during this period, it was Liddell who carried the side to the brink of promotion as they finished third, third, fourth, fourth and third again in the closing years of the 1950s. They just needed something to give them a final push back into the big time. That something was called Bill Shankly.

Billy Liddell (1938–61)

LIVERPOOL have always prized the team ethic above individual glory. Although Billy Liddell was the modest epitome of that creed, he was such an influential figure that the club was popularly known as "Liddellpool" during his time at Anfield: and few other players are as worthy of legendary status as the flying winger who could outscore almost all centre-forwards.

Skill, speed, strength and versatility were his greatest assets. He could beat opponents with either his pace or ball control — or simply muscle his way past them on his way to the bye-line. Equally at home on either flank, he actually played in every outfield position during his 23 years at the club. Liddell had a lethal shot which accounted for the majority of his 229 goals for Liverpool — still the fourth-highest total in the club's history. He even top-scored in all but one of nine seasons in the 1950s, despite being 32 when the Reds were relegated.

A supreme athlete and a model professional on and off the field, Liddell was cruelly neglected by the Scotland selectors, but a truer measure of his international stature is provided by his presence as one of only two men to play in both the Great Britain sides which faced the Rest of Europe and the Rest of the World in 1947 — the other being Stanley Matthews. At Anfield, he remains to many the greatest player the club has ever seen.

Born: 10 January, 1922, Dunfermline, Scotland
Height/weight: 5ft 10in/12st 11lb
Position: Forward
Games: 536
Goals: 229
Previous clubs: None
Honours: League Championship 1946-47
International status: Scotland international

Flying winger Billy Liddell spent over 20 years at Liverpool and scored 229 goals during his career

The 1960s

AFTER half a decade of decline it took Bill Shankly just two seasons to revolutionise Liverpool Football Club and restore them to the top flight — and just two more to make them champions of England.

1960—61 saw the Reds miss out on promotion by a single place yet again. But Shankly had seen what was required to make the difference, and once he had signed Ian St John and Ron Yeats the second-division title was soon on its way to Anfield. They topped the table throughout 1961—62, amassed a club record 62 points, scored a best-ever 99 goals and were unbeaten at home. Striker Roger Hunt found the net 41 times in 41 league games — a record that still stands today. The ecstatic fans loved them and in the gleeful celebrations that followed the confirmation of their return to the top flight, St John and Yeats had to be rescued by police from the sea of supporters that engulfed the Anfield pitch.

Liverpool did not start well on their first season back in the big-time, losing more than half of their first 15 games. But they were quick learners, and shot up the table on the back of a spell of nine wins in succession. The Reds finally finished eighth — after beating Spurs 5—2 on Good Friday and losing to them 7—2 on Easter Monday — and reached the semi-finals of the FA Cup. That was a promising start — and things were to get better and better.

Shankly added Peter Thompson to his squad for the start of the 1963—64 season and his Championship jigsaw was complete. With the new winger's skill on the left complementing Callaghan's directness down the right, and Hunt and St John feeding off their high-quality crosses, the Reds scored 92 goals in taking the title, putting six past Wolves, Stoke, Sheffield United and Ipswich, and hitting five against Aston Villa. But the sweetest victory was the one that put them on the brink of the Championship, a 3—0 win over a Manchester United side that would finish runners-up and contained the likes of Best, Law and Charlton. Liverpool needed just four points from their last five games to take the league title, and sealed their triumph with a 5—0 Anfield hammering of Arsenal, inspired appropriately by Peter Thompson.

1964—65 saw Shankly's team dip to seventh in the

Inspirational Liverpool skipper Ron Yeats shows off the 1964–65 Championship to the fans

Roger Hunt brought glory and goals to the Reds

table, but bringing home the club's first FA Cup in its 73-year history proved more than adequate compensation. The following season, 1965—66, Liverpool romped to the Championship again and were runners-up in the European Cup-winners' Cup. Using just 14 players all term, they topped the table before Christmas and lost only two of their last 19 games to wrap up the title with a game to spare. Although they were one of the most entertaining of all Liverpool sides, they also conceded just 34 goals all season.

However, those three seasons were to represent the peak of Shankly's first great side, and their grip on English football slackened throughout the remaining four years of the decade as the manager delayed in phasing out the now-ageing players who had served him so well. Hunt continued to score regularly, hitting 25 goals in 1967—68, but despite making new signings in Tony Hateley and Alun Evans, Liverpool could not regain their crown. They never finished out of the top five but managed second only once, in 1968—69. An overhaul, Shankly decided, was overdue.

Roger Hunt (1959–70)

THE goalscoring record of Roger Hunt bears comparison with that of any striker of any era. Even the great Ian Rush could not deprive him of all his Liverpool records.

Blessed with explosive acceleration and an equally violent shot, Hunt scored on his debut as a 21-year-old and went on to net 285 times in 489 appearances. Rush eventually passed that figure but Hunt's total of 245 League goals remains unsurpassed, as does his seasonal best of 41 goals in 41 games. No Liverpool player — Rush and Robbie Fowler included — has reached their half-century of strikes as quickly as did the ice-cool finisher from Golborne, who topped the Reds' goalscoring charts in nine of his ten seasons at the club.

Hunt was never showy in his skills, but possessed the raw physical power that could buy him vital time and space in front of goal. His goals powered Liverpool to their first FA Cup success in 1965 as well as to the Championships that flanked the Wembley win. During the mid-60s, he was almost unstoppable on the domestic scene and proved just as dangerous at international level.

Hunt scored 18 goals in his 34 games for England and helped his country win the World Cup in 1966. He scored vital goals in the tournament's early rounds and his work-rate was a crucial influence on the final itself. However, Hunt was — wrongly — believed to have taken national hero Jimmy Greaves's place in the side, and under public persecution for this crime he quit the international game a couple of years later. His standing at Anfield remains unaltered, however, where he will always be remembered as "Sir" Roger Hunt.

Born: 20 July, 1938, Golborne, Lancashire
Height: 5ft 9in
Weight: 12st 1lb
Position: Forward
Games: 489
Goals: 285
Previous clubs: None
Honours: World Cup 1966; League Championship 1963—64, 1965—66; FA Cup 1964—65
International status: England international

The 1970s

BILL Shankly was the architect of Liverpool's successes of the early 1970s, but the catalyst for the Reds' rise to the top once more was the lesser-known Barry Endean. For the third division centre-forward's header which gave Watford a shock FA Cup victory over the Reds in February 1970 prompted the Anfield manager to break up his old team almost on the spot.

By the start of the 1970—71 campaign the likes of Ray Clemence, Larry Lloyd, Alun Evans, John Toshack and Alec Lindsay were replacing such famous names as Lawrence, St John, Yeats, Hunt and Strong, and although they finished only fifth in the League they beat their own record for the fewest goals conceded by shipping just 24 all term.

As in 1963, Liverpool were just one player away from becoming an irresistible footballing force. This time the missing link was Kevin Keegan, who arrived from Scunthorpe just before the 1971 FA Cup Final defeat and quickly became the racing heartbeat of the Reds' attack. The last day of the 1971—72 season saw Liverpool needing to win at Arsenal to claim the Championship. And when Toshack tucked away Keegan's precision pass just a few minutes from the end they thought they had done it — only for an offside decision to destroy the dream.

But 12 months later a rampaging Liverpool could not be denied either at home or abroad. In 1972—73 they brought home the Championship and UEFA Cup, while also reaching the quarter-finals of the League Cup. The Reds lost just two matches before the turn of the year, were defeated at home only once all season and failed to score on only four occasions. Their record eighth title was clinched on Easter Monday before yet another Anfield full house, with a 2—0 win over Leeds United.

This, however, was only the beginning. The following season Liverpool won their second FA Cup to mark Shankly's farewell season, and once Bob Paisley had taken a year to emerge from his predecessor's shadow he put the club on course for domination of England and Europe. The 1975—76 Championship was won by a last-day win at Wolves, and was swiftly joined in the Anfield trophy room by the UEFA Cup. The next season, 1976—77, was arguably the best of them all, as — despite a 5—1 crash at Aston Villa — an undefeated home record helped Paisley's team retain the title and reach the finals of the FA Cup and European Cups. The Reds lost at Wembley but won in

There will only ever be one Bill Shankly – sharp, articulate and witty, the Scot was idolized by everyone connected with Liverpool FC

Rome to give the club its most famous of all triumphs.

That coronation as champions of Europe was to be Kevin Keegan's farewell performance, but Liverpool had the worthiest of replacements lined up. Kenny Dalglish arrived from Celtic to hit 20 goals in 42 games in 1977—78 and, most importantly, score the winner which retained the European Cup.

1978—79 began with a 7—0 thrashing of Spurs and an early departure from the European Cup concentrated Anfield minds on the League. Not only did they go on to win their 11th title, but they did so with a record 68 points and by conceding just 16 goals, an all-time low that is unlikely ever to be matched. That figure would have been even better but for the three goals they let in at Aston Villa, in one of only four defeats all season. At home, they were unbeaten once more and ended up eight points clear of the field. The decade ended with the now-familiar sight of Liverpool topping the final table once more. Again they were undefeated at Anfield, where they conceded only eight goals. Their record Championship haul now stood at 12.

Kevin Keegan (1971–77)

FEW players have made as big an impact on a football club as Kevin Keegan did at Liverpool. The scouts who spotted him for the Reds in 1971 had actually gone to Scunthorpe to watch another player, but it was the little striker who caught their eye. He continued to do so in training from the moment he arrived at Anfield and became one of the few young players to by-pass a lengthy learning spell in the reserves.

Keegan was pitched into the first team at just 20, and scored inside 12 minutes of his debut. He played with a passion and determination equal to those of his manager, and in just over 12 months had become an England international. His burning pace and impeccable control at speed were his most obvious attributes, but it was his incredible energy and verve that made him the superstar he quickly became. Stockily-built and with a low centre of gravity, he was a handful in even the tightest of spaces and his courage made him almost impossible to shake off. Even in the air there was no escaping him, although only five feet eight would regularly outjump the giant centre-backs he was up against.

His partnership with John Toshack made Liverpool one of the most feared teams in Europe; and although the pairing is best remembered for the towering Welshman winning headers for his partner to finish off, Keegan returned the favour often enough himself. His goals helped win the 1974 FA Cup and the 1976 UEFA Cup, and his running ragged of the great Berti Vogts was the decisive influence on the 1977 European Cup final against German side Borussia Moenchengladbach. It was his finest performance in a Liverpool shirt, and the finest manner in which to leave the club.

Born: 14 February, 1951, Doncaster
Height: 5ft 8in
Weight: 10st 10lb
Position: Forward
Games: 321
Goals: 100
Other clubs: Scunthorpe United, SV Hamburg, Southampton, Newcastle United
Transfer fee: £35,000
Honours: European Cup 1976—77; League Championship 1972—73, 1975—76, 1976—77; UEFA Cup 1972—73, 1975—76; FA Cup 1973—74
International status: England international

Kevin Keegan is brought down by Borussia Moenchengladbach defender Bertie Vogts during the 1977 European Cup Final

Dreadful haircut, brilliant player

The 1980s

NOT content with having been the team of the 1970s, Liverpool went on to be the team of the 1980s as well, both at home and abroad. Under Bob Paisley, Joe Fagan and Kenny Dalglish they won an astonishing 14 major trophies in 10 years.

Injuries forced the Reds into using 23 players in 1980—81, and with 17 games drawn they could finish only fifth in the table. But ample compensation came in the form of a third European Cup triumph and a first success in the League Cup. The following term, with Dalglish forming a lethal striking partnership with the up-and-coming Ian Rush, Liverpool reaffirmed their almost total dominance of the English game. By Boxing Day they had won only six games and were lounging in mid-table. But the Reds then hit their stride, Rush scored his first hat-trick for the club and by Easter they were top. Their traditional strong finish — this time in a closing run of 13 wins and three draws from their last 16 matches — made sure of Championship number 13 to go alongside another League Cup.

In Paisley's final season, Liverpool turned the title race into a procession. They went top at the end of October and celebrated by hammering Everton 5—0 at Goodison, with Rush scoring four. He hit another hat-trick against Notts County as the Reds remained out on their own for the rest of the season. Although they finished 11 points clear, the winning margin would have been far greater had they not failed to win a single one of their last seven games. Liverpool could not give Paisley the FA Cup as a retirement present, but he had a third successive League Cup to go with his sixth Championship.

Joe Fagan took over where Paisley left off and helped Liverpool become only the third club in history to win three consecutive League titles. He also added the European Cup and League Cup to the trophy cabinet in 1983–84 in an unprecedented treble. A slow start was now becoming the norm, but the Reds soon floated to the top and remained largely in pole position from November onwards. After scoring 30 times in each of the previous two Championship wins, Rush now hit 48 goals in the 64 games he played in the treble-winning campaign. The Welsh international put five past Luton, four past Coventry and three past Aston Villa as he claimed the prestigious 'golden boot' award as Europe's top striker.

Inspirational skipper Graeme Souness had moved to Sampdoria in the summer of 1984 and, although they finished runners-up in both the League and European Cup the following season, Liverpool missed his iron presence in midfield. When new manager Kenny Dalglish found a suitable replacement in Steve McMahon early in the 1985—86 season, the good times rolled again. Liverpool lost to Everton in February, but a run of 11 wins and a draw from the final 12 games that followed the derby defeat closed the gap and saw the title won at Chelsea on the campaign's last day. A week later Liverpool beat Everton in the FA Cup Final to clinch the famous double.

The following term the Reds again made their way to the top of the table, but after losing the League Cup Final to Arsenal, five defeats in the final nine games saw Everton pull clear. Rush moved to Juventus in the summer of 1987 and was replaced by John Barnes and Peter Beardsley in one of the most exciting of all Anfield teams. They went 29 games unbeaten from the start of the season, lost just twice all season, scored five against Nottingham Forest and Sheffield Wednesday, and put four past Coventry (twice),

Bob Paisley was the most successful manager in the history of the English game

Newcastle (twice), Derby, Portsmouth, QPR and Watford (twice). They equalled the highest points total record in two fewer games, but were denied a second double by a slip-up in the FA Cup Final.

Liverpool took the Cup in 1988—89 but lost the League with the last kick of a season that had been extended after the Hillsborough disaster. The campaign started badly, but an unbeaten run of 18 games stretching from early January to late May took the Reds to the verge of the title, needing only to avoid a two-goal Anfield defeat by Arsenal in the season's last game. After resuming play post-Hillsborough, Liverpool played six games in 23 days, the last of which proved too much for a team now emotionally and physically drained. Michael Thomas scored the last-minute second goal that gave the Gunners the title, but the strength Liverpool had shown in getting so close to it was the most fitting of tributes to the 96 fans who died in Sheffield.

Dalglish celebrates the 1981 European Cup win

Kenny Dalglish (1977–90)

NOT only was Kenny Dalglish the greatest player Liverpool has ever seen: he was also arguably the greatest player the British game has ever seen. The Reds paid Celtic a then-record £440,000 for him in 1977 but recouped their investment many times over in silverware.

He arrived with the unenviable task of replacing Kevin Keegan and proved he was up to the task by scoring after seven minutes on his debut. He ended the 1977—78 season with 30 goals from 59 games, including the imperious chip that won the European Cup. He went on to become the only man to score a century of goals in both Scotland and England, and is his country's most capped player and joint record goalscorer. As a player he won three European Cups, six Championships, four League Cups and an FA Cup, and was ever-present with Liverpool in five of his first six seasons.

Dalglish was at his most dangerous in situations where there appeared to be little threat. Powerful enough to shield the ball from almost any challenge, and eel-like in his slippery elusiveness inside the box, he could finish from almost any position but particularly favoured cute curlers into the top corner. Although not the quickest of players, his vision and quick thinking gave him an advantage over even the paciest of opponents. The creative side of his game came most to the fore once Ian Rush appeared to lead the line and feed off the succession of chances his more senior partner created.

Dalglish became Liverpool's player-manager in 1985 and immediately led the team to the League and Cup double, scoring the goal that won the title himself. He guided the side to two more Championships and a further FA Cup before resigning under the increasing stress of the job in 1991.

Born: 4 March, 1951. Glasgow
Height: 5ft 8in
Weight: 11st 13lb
Position: Forward
Games: 497
Goals: 168
Previous club: Celtic
Transfer fee: £440,000
Honours: European Cup 1977—78, 1980—81, 1983—84; League Championship 1978—79, 1979—80, 1981—82, 1982—83, 1983—84, 1985—86 (as manager 1987—88, 1989—90); FA Cup 1985—86 (as manager 1988—89); League Cup 1980—81, 1981—82, 1982—83, 1983—84
International status: Scotland international

To the Dawn of the Premiership years

The 1990s arrived in much the same fashion as had the '80s before them. But this time initial success was to prove anything but an indicator of what was to follow.

At the start of the 1989—90 season, Kenny Dalglish decided he preferred Ian Rush to John Aldridge in his attack and the latter man quickly moved on to Real Sociedad of Spain, albeit not before making one last memorable substitute's appearance. On September 12, Liverpool played Crystal Palace and had to lock the gates on a capacity crowd long before kick-off. Those who could not get in missed an astounding 9—0 victory, in which Aldridge was sent on late in the game to convert a farewell penalty in front of the Kop, to whom he later gifted his shirt and boots. Eight players got on the scoresheet to sound the loudest of Championship warnings that night, although Palace would gain their revenge in the FA Cup semi-final.

Five defeats in eight games during October and November appeared to derail their challenge, but the illusion was only fleeting. From December 2, they lost just one more League game all term and took the title on the back of an avalanche of goals from late-season loan signing Ronnie Rosenthal. The Reds clinched their 18th Championship with a 1—0 Anfield win over Derby, in which Dalglish made his last competitive appearance as a late substitute.

His team celebrated in style by travelling to Coventry on the campaign's last day, and after conceding a goal in the opening minutes ran riot to score six times without reply themselves, three of which gave top-scorer John Barnes his first Liverpool hat-trick. But that 1990 triumph was the last sight of the Championship trophy Anfield would get for a long, long time.

The first division of the Football League had just two more seasons as the country's top flight before being supplanted by the Premiership, and Liverpool could lift the title in neither. For a long time, however, they looked as though they would. With Rush, Barnes and Beardsley all scoring freely, the Reds opened the 1990—91 campaign with eight straight victories, including a 3—2 thriller at Everton and a 4—0 thrashing of Manchester United featuring

the cheekiest of hat-tricks from Beardsley. As they reached game 14 without defeat, the record run of 1987—88 looked in danger, only for the first signs of manager Dalglish's growing uncertainty to send them to a 3—0 defeat at Arsenal. Liverpool's form faltered as the boss started altering his teamsheet according to the opposition, and eyebrows were raised at the purchases of Jimmy Carter and David Speedie, although the fact that the latter man scored three times in his first two games, against Manchester United and Everton, calmed the fans' fears somewhat.

Then, after the epic 4—4 FA Cup draw at Goodison, Dalglish dropped the bombshell of his resignation. Ronnie Moran took charge until Graeme Souness arrived in April, and although the Reds won just four out of nine games in that period they were still in touch with rivals Arsenal on the run-in. Souness's first two games were won 3—0, but defeats at Chelsea and then Nottingham Forest finished Liverpool's challenge with a game to play.

In 1991—92 the Reds won the FA Cup but were rarely in the hunt in the League. They scored more than two goals in a game only twice, and finished a distant sixth after drawing as many games as they won. Their only consolation came in depriving Manchester United of the title by beating them 2—0 in Anfield's last game of the season. A change of competition would not bring the Reds an immediate change of fortune.

Liverpool's Michael Thomas leads Manchester United's Andrei Kanchelskis a merry dance during a 1992 match

Alan Hansen (1977–91)

ALAN Hansen's long and illustrious career was ended by a persistent knee injury in 1991, but his reputation as one of the finest defenders ever to play the game will survive for ever.

The tall, graceful Scot was the star of Liverpool's defence for almost a decade and a half, a period in which he garnered an incredible 16 major honours and captained the team to the League and Cup double. Signed from Partick Thistle in 1977, he played in the European Cup final at 22 and the following season ousted Emlyn Hughes from a defence that conceded a record low of just 16 League goals. But while he had both the skill and the confidence to achieve such precocious feats, the latter quality at first terrorised his team-mates as he calmly dribbled his way out of the defensive maelstrom. It wasn't long, however, before they had an equal belief in his ability, for the unflappable Hansen's forays forward became a prime source of Liverpool attacks through the '80s and into the '90s.

He rarely ventured all the way to his opponents' box, but in his own penalty area he was without peer, winning tackle after tackle with a perfectly-timed extension of one of his apparently-telescopic legs. His only flaw was, perhaps, a vulnerability in the air, but his impeccable reading of the play more than compensated for that minor shortcoming.

A knee injury picked up in 1980 began to trouble Hansen towards the end of that decade, and he was out of action for most of the 1988—89 campaign after undergoing surgery on the joint. He missed only seven games as the Championship returned to Anfield the following season but was not fit enough to start the 1990—91 term and eventually announced his retirement. Few, if any, players have been as sorely missed.

Born: 13 June, 1955, Alloa, Scotland
Height: 6ft 1in
Weight: 13st
Position: Defender
Games: 607
Goals: 13
Previous club: Partick Thistle
Transfer fee: £100,000
Honours: European Cup 1977—78, 1980—81, 1983—84; League Championship 1978—79, 1979—80, 1981—82, 1982—83, 1983—84, 1985—86, 1987—88, 1989—90; FA Cup 1985—86, 1987—88; League Cup 1980—81, 1982—83, 1983—84
International status: Scotland international

Alan Hansen takes centre stage as Liverpool collect the 1989–90 Championship title

The Premiership Years

For so long the undisputed kings of the old Division One, Liverpool have taken time to adjust to the demands of the Premiership

The Premiership era has been one of more pain than gain for Liverpool Football Club. From an optimistic dawn to the nadir of Graeme Souness's final months as manager and then a partial revival under Roy Evans, the bottom line remains that the Reds' first five years in the renamed top flight condemned them to their longest wait for the title since before Bill Shankly arrived at Anfield.

When the FA Premiership began in 1992, Liverpool were hopeful of bringing the new trophy to Anfield at the first time of asking, despite having just experienced an often turbulent debut campaign for boss Souness. Yet the stability and progress for which everyone at Anfield was praying failed to materialize and, by their own dizzying standards, the Reds endured a miserable decline that ultimately brought the volatile Scot's stewardship to an end.

In 1992–93, Liverpool were worryingly reliant on Ian Rush, but still found the back of the net far more often than they had the previous term. However, with injury problems and poor form in defence they also conceded more goals and although they finished sixth for the second successive year, the position flattered them. They won only one more game than they lost and relied on a late run to lift them from seventh last with only two months of the season to go. For the first time in almost 30

Steve McManaman after the 1995 Coca–Cola Cup

years, they had failed to qualify for Europe.

That disappointment was expected to spell the end for Souness, but he was given a stay of execution and bought Nigel Clough and Neil Ruddock in a bid to boost his attack and beef up the defence for the 1993–94 campaign. But, again decimated by injury and racked by dressing room unrest, Liverpool performed unconvincingly and with no sign of discernable improvement in the league, a shock FA Cup defeat saw club and manager part company. Assistant boss Roy Evans stepped up to take charge but the Reds' slide continued through the remainder of the season. This time they finished eighth, their worst final position since their first season back in the top flight, in 1962–63.

Eager to see Evans succeed, the fans were happy to blame the sorry mess Souness had bequeathed him for that continued decline, and once the new man began to mould his own side the following season, the situation began to stabilize. Evans made no major signings in the summer but within a month of the 1994–95 season kicking off he had plunged into the transfer market to buy centre-backs Phil Babb and John Scales.

Flanking Ruddock, they formed a three-man central defence around which the manager developed a system of wing-backs pushing up from defence to give width to a three-man central midfield. The formation was an initial success, bringing Liverpool the League Cup and giving them the second meanest defence in the Premiership. With Robbie Fowler established as a top-class striker alongside Rush, they moved up to finish fourth and got back into European competition.

Further progress was made the following year, 1995–96, although the season ended in the bitter disappointment of an FA Cup final defeat by arch-rivals Manchester United. With Rush heading for the twilight of his Anfield career, Evans had paid a British record fee in the summer of 1995 to partner Stan Collymore with Robbie Fowler. The pair did not always hit it off but, with the wing-back system modified to give Steve McManaman the floating role in which he became the Premiership's most dangerous attacker, the Reds scored freely as the Fowler-Collymore axis became the most productive strike-force in England.

But while a collection of scintillating displays against their title rivals showed Liverpool to be the finest footballing side in the country, they could not produce a similar standard of consistency. A "Black November" when they lost valuable ground in the league, coupled with an inability to see off the division's strugglers, cost them the title, although they moved up a final place to third.

The arrival of the 1996-97 season brought great expectations back to Anfield, only for the campaign to end if not in hard times then certainly with even more frustrating feelings of underachievement. Fowler continued to score freely, but the uncertainty that had afflicted Liverpool defences throughout the '90s resurfaced to cost them a Premiership crown they knew was theirs for the taking. The Reds looked in pole position for two thirds of the race only to fade so dramatically in the final furlongs that they slipped back to fourth, and missed out on not only the chance to scratch their seven-year Championship itch, but also the European Cup place that a runners-up spot would have clinched.

It was to the credit of Evans and his team that within two years of what to many had seemed like the onset of possibly terminal decline, failing to win the League was again being seen as a major disappointment. But Liverpool had reached a Premiership plateau. Now equipping the club for another final ascent to the summit would be an even harder challenge than the ship-steadying task the manager had first been handed.

Veteran striker Ian Rush battles for possession with Sheffield Wednesday's Des Walker

Season 1992–93

AUG 16: Liverpool give a debut to £1m goalkeeper David James in the first League game televised live by BSkyB, but a Teddy Sheringham goal condemns them to their only opening day defeat since 1981 as they go down 1–0 at Nottingham Forest.

SEPT 10: Dean Saunders is sold to Aston Villa for £2.3 million, just over a season after arriving from Derby County for £2.9 million. He scored 11 league goals in 42 games.

OCT 18: Ian Rush passes Roger Hunt's Liverpool scoring record when his 287th goal gives the Reds a 2-0 lead at Old Trafford. But after a foul on Jan Molby puts the midfield maestro out of the game, Manchester United snatch a point through a late equalizer from Mark Hughes. With just three wins from their first 12 games Liverpool lie 16th in the table, just three points above the relegation zone.

NOV 7: Rush scores his 200th League goal for Liverpool in a 4-1 home win over Middlesbrough.

DECEMBER 13: Liverpool bounce back from Merseyside derby defeat to spoil Kenny Dalglish's Anfield homecoming. A brace from Mark Walters gives the Reds a 2–1 win over Dalglish's Blackburn Rovers that leaves them ninth in the table, 11 points off the pace.

DECEMBER 16: Crystal Palace end the Reds' League Cup interest at the fourth-round stage with a winner in extra-time.

DECEMBER 19: New signing Stig Inge Bjornebye has the misfortune to make his debut in a Liverpool team that crashes to its worst defeat in 16 years. The Norwegian takes the Man of the Match award and hits a post, but the sending-off of goalscorer Jamie Redknapp sees outnumbered Liverpool collapse to a 5–1 loss as Coventry run out 5–1 winners.

JAN 13: The pressure on Souness increases as First Division Bolton Wanderers outplay Liverpool at Anfield to win an FA Cup third–round replay 2–0.

JAN 31: After a week of team crisis meetings and morale–boosting sessions, Liverpool end a run of seven games without a win by beating Arsenal at Highbury courtesy of a Barnes penalty. James marks his return to the side with a superb spot–kick save from Paul Merson, while the Gunners' Nigel Winterburn is sent off for two fouls on Steve McManaman. The Reds remain 12th in the table.

FEB 8: A recall to the England squad for John Barnes is the only bright spot in a month when Liverpool go six games without a win.

MARCH 21: Liverpool have picked up with three straight wins, including derby victory over Everton, but the injury crisis that forces Souness to use 25 play-

David James denies Paul Merson from the penalty spot during the clash with Arsenal in January 1993

ers during the campaign reaches its gravest proportions. Reserve team coach Sammy Lee, aged 34, is named in the squad that travels to Crystal Palace.

MARCH 22: The Reds draw 1–1 at Selhurst Park but Souness is shown the red card from the dug-out for allegedly swearing at a linesman. He quickly faces an FA disrepute charge.

MAY 4: After more mediocre form, Souness misses training before a second marathon Anfield board meeting in 48 hours sparks speculation that he is heading for the sack as the club drifts towards its worst finish in more than 20 years.

MAY 5: The Liverpool manager vows that he will not quit the post. Later, Don Hutchison becomes the sixth Liverpool player of the season to be sent off when he is dismissed for elbowing during a 3–2 defeat at lowly Oldham, a result that is widely expected to sound the death knell for Souness's stewardship.

MAY 8: Rush scores his 300th goal for the Reds in a 6–2 closing day victory over Tottenham Hotspur as Liverpool finish sixth, albeit 25 points off the top and after losing 15 games. Souness is not at Anfield and is spotted watching Coventry play Leeds.

MAY 9: At an extraordinary Anfield press conference, rather than announcing the anticipated departure of Souness, chairman David Moores reveals that he is to be given the chance to see out the remaining three years of his managerial contract. Director Tony Ensor resigns over the decision, while Roy Evans is appointed assistant manager. Souness survives to fight another day.

May 1993 and Ian Rush rounds the Tottenham 'keeper to score his 300th goal for Liverpool

Season 1993–94

JUN 19: Nigel Clough, a £2,275,000 summer buy from Nottingham Forest, scores both goals in a 2–0 opening day win over Sheffield Wednesday, for whom Carlton Palmer is dismissed for a crude tackle after just 13 minutes.

August 22: A 5–0 win at newcomers Swindon Town puts Liverpool top of the League on goal difference. Double marksman Steve McManaman scores his first – and last – goals of the season.

SEPTEMBER 17: Eyebrows are raised by the signing of West Ham hard-man Julian Dicks in a swap deal worth £1.6 million that sees Mike Marsh and David Burrows move south.

Nigel Clough made a dream start for Liverpool, scoring both goals against Sheffield Wednesday

SEPTEMBER 19: McManaman and Grobbelaar almost come to blows after Everton's first goal in a 2–0 derby win for the Blues. The defeat is the third of four straight losses that see Liverpool fall from top spot.

OCTOBER 2: Liverpool stop the rot with a 0–0 draw against Arsenal but go a fifth game without scoring.

OCTOBER 16: The Anfield goal drought is ended in spectacular fashion by the introduction of Robbie Fowler. After scoring six times in the League Cup against Fulham – including five on his home debut – the 18–year–old scores on his Premiership debut to help the Reds beat Oldham 2–1.

OCTOBER 28: Video evidence clears Ruddock of an FA misconduct charge after he was accused of punching Mike Newell in a brawl at Blackburn six weeks earlier.

OCTOBER 30: Fowler hits his first Premiership hat–trick in a 4–2 Anfield win over Southampton. Liverpool lie seventh, 14 points off the pace.

DECEMBER 11: Mark Wright saves his team's blushes with an 86th minute equalizer that prevents bottom club Swindon from snatching an incredible 2–1 Anfield win.

DECEMBER 14: Liverpool leave the League Cup at Selhurst Park at the same stage for the second year running. This time they lose to Wimbledon in a penalty shoot–out .

JANUARY 4: Liverpool stage one of the greatest fightbacks in their history when they recover from being 3–0 down after 23 minutes against Manchester United to snatch a draw through goals from Clough (two), and Ruddock.

JANUARY 21: Fowler is found to have a cracked bone in his leg that keeps him out for two months.

JANUARY 25: Second Division Bristol City pull off a shock 1–0 win at Anfield to condemn Liverpool to a second successive third–round FA Cup exit at the hands of lower League opposition.

JANUARY 28: Graeme Souness resigns as Liverpool manager after less than two years in charge, with the team lying fifth in the League. He says: "The fans have been very patient, but now I feel their patience is running out."

JANUARY 31: Liverpool appoint assistant manager and boot–room stalwart Roy Evans as Souness's successor, handing him a two-and-a-half-year contract.

FEBRUARY 19: Injury to ever–present Bruce Grobbelaar at Leeds allows David James back into the team and effectively ends the Zimbabwean keeper's tenure as Anfield's last line of defence.

FEBRUARY 26: An Ian Rush goal against Coventry gives Evans his first managerial victory, at the fourth attempt.

MARCH 5: Liverpool lose their next game, at

Blackburn, but go on to beat Everton 2–1 in the Anfield derby through a winner from boyhood Blues fan Fowler. Rush is, as usual, the other Reds scorer.

APRIL 2: Sheffield United win at Anfield for the first time in 21 years as Liverpool reel from back–to–back defeats at Arsenal and Manchester United.

APRIL 30: Norwich City are the party poopers as they win 1–0 at Anfield in the last game to be played in front of the Spion Kop terrace. Jeremy Goss scores the winner.

MAY 7: Liverpool finish with two more defeats to end the season in eighth place, their worst final placing in more than 30 years. The silver lining is in the form of youngsters Jamie Redknapp and Steve McManaman, and Fowler's 12 League goals in 27 starts. Rush scores 13 in 41, while no player appears in every game.

End of an era as the Kop stages its last performance in a League match against Norwich in April 1994

Season 1994–95

AUGUST 20: Liverpool hit promoted Crystal Palace for six on the opening day. Steve McManaman scores twice in the 6–1 win – 363 days on from his last goals for the club.

AUGUST 28: Robbie Fowler scores the fastest hat-trick in Premiership history. Arsenal are the victims of a four-minute, 33-second blast that puts Liverpool top of the League.

SEPTEMBER 1: World Cup star Phil Babb signs from Coventry City for £3.75 million, a record for a defender. Roy Evans follows up by capturing Wimbledon's £3m centre-half John Scales just 24 hours later.

SEPTEMBER 24: Liverpool unveil a new-look formation based around the three centre-backs Scales, Ruddock and Babb, flanked by attacking wing-backs Rob Jones and Stig Inge Bjornebye. The ploy works as Liverpool end Newcastle's 100% record with a 1–1 draw on Tyneside that flatters the hosts rather than the visitors.

OCTOBER 1: McManaman appears to have grabbed his first senior hat-trick with second-half goals in a 4–1 win against Sheffield Wednesday, only for one of his efforts to be credited as a Des Walker own-goal afterwards.

OCTOBER 11: Two days after McManaman is elevated to the senior England squad, Jamie Redknapp hits a hat-trick for the country's under-21s in Austria. Robbie Fowler, however, is sent off in the same game for dissent.

Steve McManaman walks off with the ball under his shirt after his two goals against Sheffield Wednesday

OCTOBER 29: A 3–1 win at Ipswich keeps Liverpool in touch with League leaders Newcastle. The Reds lie fifth, six points off the pace but with a game in hand.

NOVEMBER 11: A 3–1 win over Chelsea puts the Reds third but the big news of the week is that the police and FA are to investigate newspaper claims that Bruce Grobbelaar took bribes to throw matches while playing at Liverpool.

NOVEMBER 16: Ruddock and McManaman make their England debuts in the 1–0 friendly win over Nigeria.

DECEMBER 26: Fowler scores a penalty to help Liverpool to a 2–1 Boxing Day win at Leicester City but finds himself on an FA charge after hitching up his shorts to bare his backside at home supporters.

JANUARY 20: Steve Nicol ends 13 years of Anfield service by becoming player-coach of Notts County.

JANUARY 24: Roy Evans criticises Everton's roughhouse tactics as Joe Royle's 'Dogs of War' grind out a 0–0 draw at Anfield.

FEBRUARY 1: Sir John Smith, former Liverpool chairman and driving force behind the scenes throughout the glory years of the 1970s and '80s, dies aged 74.

FEBRUARY 25: Liverpool end an underachieving run of four games without victory by beating Sheffield Wednesday 2–1 at Hillsborough. They go fourth in the table, 15 points adrift of top spot.

MARCH 4: The Reds brush title pretenders Newcastle United aside with a majestic 2–0 Anfield win superbly engineered by Jamie Redknapp.

MARCH 11: Liverpool lose 2–1 to Spurs in the FA Cup quarter-final thanks to a late Jurgen Klinsmann winner.

MARCH 19: Redknapp scores the opener in another impressive win that dents Manchester United's Championship ambitions and rekindles Liverpool's hopes. A late Steve Bruce own-goal seals a 2–0 win.

MARCH 21: Liverpool sign Ireland Under-21 winger Mark Kennedy from Millwall for a basic £1.5 million

Roy Evans contemplates life as manager as he attempts to bring the League title back to Liverpool

with another £500,000 to follow according to appearances.

APRIL 2: A superb display from Steve McManaman capped by two fine goals wins Liverpool the League Cup with a 2–1 Wembley win over Bolton Wanderers.

APRIL 5: Stig Inge Bjornebye breaks his leg in a 3–1 defeat of Southampton after catching his studs in the turf while stretching for a cross in front of goal.

APRIL 9: Robbie Fowler is named PFA Young Footballer of the Year.

MAY 14: Liverpool beat Blackburn 2–1 at Anfield on the season's final day with a last-minute free-kick from Jamie Redknapp. But Rovers are still crowned champions as Manchester United can only draw at West Ham. Liverpool finish fourth, 15 points off the pace. Fowler is top scorer with 32 goals from 57 games. James and Fowler are the only ever-presents in the side.

Season 1995–96

AUGUST 19: £8.5 million British record signing, Stan Collymore scores the winner on his Premiership debut as his 20-yard curler gives the Reds a 1–0 opening day win over Sheffield Wednesday at Anfield.

AUGUST 26: Injury to Collymore gives Robbie Fowler, dropped by Roy Evans over a perceived attitude problem in pre-season training, his first start of the season. He scores with an outstanding volley in 3–1 win at Spurs. John Barnes gets the other two to break the 100 goals barrier for Liverpool.

SEPTEMBER 6: Liverpool pay Bolton Wanderers £4.5 million for midfielder Jason McAteer.

SEPTEMBER 9: Liverpool suffer their first defeat of the season as a Phil Babb own goal condemns them to a 1–0 defeat at Wimbledon. Vinnie Jones is sent off for an apparent butt on Collymore, although the dismissal is later overturned on appeal.

Robbie Fowler destroys Bolton Wanderers with a four goal haul as the Reds win 5–2

SEPTEMBER 23: Robbie Fowler scores four goals in a 5–2 Anfield demolition of Bolton that puts the Reds third in the Premiership.

OCTOBER 1: Fowler scores two superb goals as Liverpool draw 2–2 at Manchester United, although the Reds' performance is overshadowed by Eric Cantona's return to football after his long ban for a kung-fu kick attack on a Crystal Palace fan.

OCTOBER 31: A late goal from Brondby's Dan Eggen at Anfield puts Liverpool out of the UEFA Cup and heralds the onset of 'Black November'.

NOVEMBER 11: Stan Collymore is fined an estimated £24,000 for criticising the club in a magazine interview.

NOVEMBER 14: Jamie Redknapp tears a hamstring after just six minutes of England's friendly match against Switzerland and is out for four months.

NOVEMBER 29: Elimination from the League Cup rounds off a miserable month in which the Reds lose at both Newcastle and Middlesbrough, and Everton gain their first Anfield League win in eight years.

DECEMBER 12: Liverpool bounce back to outclass Manchester United at Anfield, winning 2–0 through goals from Robbie Fowler. The striker follows up a week later with a classic hat-trick as Arsenal are beaten 3–1.

JANUARY 1: A comeback victory over Nottingham Forest leaves Liverpool seven points off the Premiership pace, but with a game in hand.

JANUARY 6: Ian Rush breaks Denis Law's 20th century FA Cup goalscoring record with his 42nd strike in the competition as Rochdale are seen off 7–0.

JANUARY 31: Liverpool go second in the table after a 2–0 win at Aston Villa.

FEBRUARY 14: Legendary Reds' boss Bob Paisley, the most successful manager in history, dies at the age of 77.

MARCH 2: Three goals in the first eight minutes against Aston Villa take Liverpool to within two

Jamie Redknapp is back in action for Liverpool in the 1996 FA Cup semi-final against Aston Villa

points of League leaders Manchester United.

MARCH 23: The Reds' 20–match unbeaten run ends in a 1–0 defeat at Nottingham Forest.

MARCH 31: Jamie Redknapp returns to the starting line-up for the FA Cup semi-final clash with Aston Villa. Liverpool win 3–0 in front of a crowd of under 40,000 after the FA's ticket pricing policy proves too expensive for thousands of fans.

APRIL 4: Liverpool boost their flagging title hopes with an astonishing 4–3 win over Newcastle United. Stan Collymore scores the winner deep in injury time.

APRIL 6: A 1–0 defeat at Coventry City kills off the Reds' Championship challenge. Steve Harkness is out for eight months after a tackle from John Salako breaks his leg.

APRIL 21: Robbie Fowler is third in the Football Writers' Association poll for Footballer of the Year after taking the PFA's Young Player award for the second year running.

APRIL 27: Ian Rush makes his final appearance in front of the Anfield fans and signs off with a 1–0 win over Middlesbrough, although he is unable to get his name on the scoresheet.

MAY 5: Rush scores the last of his 344 Liverpool goals as the Reds warm up for Wembley by relegating Manchester City with a 2–2 draw at Maine Road. They finish third in the League with 70 points, but are nine behind champions Manchester United.

MAY 11: The most anticipated FA Cup Final in years is a huge anti-climax as a disappointing Liverpool lose to Manchester United through a late goal from Eric Cantona.

MAY 17: The Reds gain some consolation when their junior side win the FA Youth Cup, beating West Ham 4–1 on aggregate in the final.

Season 1996–97

AUGUST 17: The Reds are pegged back three times by a Fabrizio Ravanelli hat-trick in a 3–3 draw at Middlesbrough. Stig Inge Bjornebye scores his first goal for the club.

SEPTEMBER 15: £3 million summer signing Patrik Berger scores two wonder goals at Leicester City to set up a 3–0 win that puts Liverpool top of the League.

SEPTEMBER 21: Berger scores two more in a 5–1 thrashing of Chelsea. A European goal within the week takes his tally to five in his first two and a half hours of action for his new club.

Liverpool their first home defeat in more than a year.

DECEMBER 14: Two goals for Robbie Fowler in a 5–1 hammering of Middlesbrough take him through the 100 Liverpool goals barrier. He reaches the milestone in 165 games – one fewer than it took Ian Rush to achieve the feat.

JANUARY 8: A mistake by David James dumps Liverpool out of the League Cup at Middlesbrough. The goalkeeper blames his concentration loss on an eight-hour pre-match computer games session.

JANUARY 10: Liverpool sign out-of-contract Norwegian defender Bjorn Tore Kvarme on a free from Rosenborg. He makes an impressive debut

New signing Patrik Berger scores two magnificent goals against Leicester City and gains cult status

OCTOBER 10: Liverpool suffer their first defeat of the campaign, losing unluckily 1–0 at Manchester United. They slip from first to third in the table.

NOVEMBER 6: Stan Collymore fails to appear when selected for a reserve game at Tranmere Rovers and is fined around £20,000 for his absence.

DECEMBER 7: Sheffield Wednesday pull off a coup by man-marking Steve McManaman to inflict on

against Aston Villa but is pipped to the Man of the Match award by young midfielder Jamie Carragher, who marks his first start for the club with the opening goal in a 3–0 win.

JANUARY 26: After cruising to a 2–0 half-time lead, Liverpool's defence disintegrates in the second period to send them out of the FA Cup by conceding four goals to eventual Cup winners Chelsea.

MARCH 2: Stan Collymore is substituted in a 1–0 defeat at Aston Villa and complains publicly that he is being made a scapegoat for the team's collective failings as they slip to second in the table.

MARCH 10: The 4–3 scoreline – and all the drama – of the previous season's Liverpool vs. Newcastle United clash is repeated on another incredible night at Anfield.

MARCH 24: Robbie Fowler is awarded a penalty at Arsenal after colliding with David Seaman but tries to persuade referee Gerald Ashby to change his mind, saying that the England keeper made no contact with him. Ashby sticks to his decision and although Seaman saves Fowler's weak spot-kick McAteer follows in to give the Reds a 2–1 win. Fowler later

Winners' Cup semi-final. The Reds win the Anfield return 2–0 a fortnight later but still go out on aggregate.

APRIL 16: Robbie Fowler is sent off with Everton's David Unsworth after the pair swap punches towards the end of a 1–1 draw at Goodison.

APRIL 19: A lame 3–1 home defeat by Manchester United effectively ends Liverpool's League challenge, although their rivals' stuttering form means they still have a mathematical chance until well inside the final week of the season.

MAY 5: Liverpool lose 2–1 at Wimbledon, although the introduction of 17-year-old Michael Owen almost

Robbie Fowler is awarded a controversial penalty against Arsenal after a tangle with David Seaman

receives a letter of commendation for his sportsmanship from UEFA.

APRIL 4: Liverpool's title hopes are dealt a massive blow when two late gaffes by David James hand relegation candidates Coventry City a 2–1 win at Anfield. The Reds slip to third.

APRIL 10: Liverpool are humbled 3–0 by Paris St Germain in the first leg of their European Cup

sparks a late recovery. Owen takes just 16 minutes to become Liverpool's youngest–ever scorer.

MAY 11: Despite Sheffield Wednesday losing their goalkeeper through injury and then having his replacement sent off, Liverpool can only draw 1–1 at Hillsborough. Wins for Arsenal and Newcastle condemn the Reds to a disappointing fourth place finish, although Robbie Fowler tops the 30 goals mark for the second season running.

Chapter 3
Liverpool in Europe

Liverpool are by far the most successful club in English football history – both at home and abroad. And despite the six-year ban that followed the Heysel disaster of 1985, they still stand among the greatest sides the European game has ever seen.

Liverpool score in the 1965 European Cup semi-final

The Reds' record in continental competition, for which they qualified in 22 consecutive seasons, stands at four European Cups and two UEFA Cups. They have also been runners-up in the European Cup and European Cup-Winners' Cup, while only Real Madrid and AC Milan have been crowned champions of Europe on more occasions. Among English clubs, Nottingham Forest's two Champions' Cup successes are as close as any side can come to Liverpool's remarkable record.

It took the Anfield men just 12 years to complete the journey from European novices to conquerors of the continent, and when they first faced up to their foreign adventure they were as green as it was possible to be. While the likes of Wolves were entertaining Honved and Spartak Moscow during the 1950s, Liverpool were languishing in the Second Division. And when they had ventured abroad, notably after the Second World War and again during the early '60s, it was across the Atlantic Ocean rather than the

English Channel they headed, on tours to the USA.

Yet that inexperience was well hidden when they made their competitive international debut in 1964–65 with a run that took them all the way to the semi-finals of the European Cup before losing controversially to Inter Milan. The Reds were introduced to all the tricks of the continental trade that season, but they also discovered the rigours of travel their quest involved.

Their first game in Europe was in Iceland, which was reached via a bus ride to Manchester airport, a flight to London followed by a connecting plane journey to Prestwick in Scotland and then on towards the Arctic Circle. Shankly's party set off on the journey almost immediately after returning from a Wembley draw in the Charity Shield and arrived back at Anfield just in time for their next League game. However, in comparison to some of the privations the Reds would experience on their later travels, that first trip was a five-star holiday for the squad.

One expedition behind the Iron Curtain found dressing room conditions so squalid that Shankly threatened to call the game off, while on another a shortage of toilet paper enabled a use to be found for the worthless local banknotes the players were given for expenses. But in view of some of the standards of cuisine the Reds experienced in their early days abroad, working toilets were often essential rather than luxury items.

Mysterious mauve-coloured soup appeared to be the dish of the day every day in many East European hotels, while after a final-straw trip to Trabzon in 1976 Liverpool began employing their own hoteliers and chefs to supervise all accommodation and food preparation for the team. On that occasion, although a scouting mission had taken place a couple of weeks beforehand, the hotel the Turks showed off that day was not the hovel in which the Reds actually ended up staying in prior to the match!

Continental competition may have been a source of as many anecdotes as it was of famous victories, but it also brought Liverpool their famous all-red strip. Until 1964, the Anfield side had played in red shirts and white shorts. Then, for the European Cup visit of Anderlecht, Shankly decided to change the shorts to match the shirts, because he believed an all-red kit would make his players look bigger. Whether it did or not, Liverpool beat the Belgian champions 3–0 that night and the strip has remained unchanged ever since.

The Reds' record of excellence in Europe stayed constant over the next 20 years as well. In taking the League Championship and UEFA Cup in 1973 they became the first English side to win trophies at home and abroad in the same season. They repeated the same double three years later, scooped the Championship and European Cup in 1977 and in 1984 picked up an unprecedented treble of European Cup, League Championship and League Cup. They were the first English side to win the European Cup twice and the first to retain the trophy. No team from these shores has played more matches in continental competition.

Ian Rush is the club's leading European scorer with 21 goals, while Dean Saunders holds the seasonal record of scoring nine times in the 1991–92 UEFA Cup. More recently, Robbie Fowler found the net in every round of the 1996–97 Cup-Winners' Cup as Liverpool reached the semi-final. That was their first appearance in the last four of a European competition since before Heysel.

The six-year ban the Reds endured after the Brussels disaster cost them much more than the opportunity to garner still more prized silverware. The seasons since their return from the wilderness in 1991 have been a period of re-education as a new Anfield generation has struggled to gain the knowledge and experience that underpinned the success of their predecessors. A return to semi-final status in 1997 suggested that Liverpool were on their way back, although they still had a long, long way to go to revisit the heady heights occupied in the 1970s and '80s.

The Sixties

In 1962, Liverpool emerged from their eight-year second division exile on the back of the self-belief instilled in them by their messianic manager Bill Shankly. When they picked up the Championship just two years later, the entire English game knew how well founded that faith was. And by the end of the following season, the whole of Europe had been introduced to a new footballing force that would come to dominate the entire continent.

The Reds enjoyed an easy introduction to the Champions' Cup in 1964–65 as Gordon Wallace's third-minute preliminary round goal in Reykjavik set up an 11–1 aggregate win. But Liverpool really came of age in the next round, when they beat the highly-rated Belgian champions Anderlecht 4–0 on aggregate. Two hard-fought goalless draws with Cologne then followed to force a quarter-final replay which was again drawn and had to be decided by the toss of a coin. Incredibly, when the referee flicked his coin it landed on its edge in the mud. The second attempt proved more successful and as Yeats and Smith leapt into the air, the 45,000 crowd knew exactly which way the lottery had gone.

That set up a semi-final clash with Inter Milan and one of the greatest nights in Anfield history. Inspired by a crowd still celebrating the club's first FA Cup success, Liverpool led inside four minutes through Roger Hunt. However, Inter equalized before a clever free-kick routine sent Callaghan in to regain the lead and St John then clinched a 3–1 win by tucking away a rebound.

But eight days later it was a different story amid a San Siro atmosphere that made the hysteria of Anfield look like a wake, as Inter scored three goals in the first 20 minutes. The decisive third was a classic, but the opener was scored straight from an indirect free-kick, and for the second, although Lawrence was caught out while bouncing the ball in front of goal, continental football normally took a dim view of the sort of challenge on the keeper that robbed him of the ball. Inter went on to win the cup, although years later evidence was uncovered to support the claims of Shankly that the referee had been bribed.

Either way, Liverpool had learned an important lesson and wasted little time in putting their newly acquired knowledge to good effect. Their next continental outing gave them revenge of a sort as they beat Juventus 2–1 in the first round of the 1965–66 Cup-Winners' Cup. The Reds went on to reach the final by beating Celtic in a thrilling semi. Having lost 1–0 in Glasgow to the side that the following year would become the first British team to win the European Cup, Liverpool came through at Anfield when Geoff Strong defied a cartilage injury that saw him play most of the game with a piece of rope holding his knee in place to head the second goal in a 2–0 win.

Liverpool lost the final 2–1 to Borussia Dortmund but were back in the Champions' Cup the following term. However, this time they met with their heaviest European defeat in only round two, when they had the misfortune to meet the legendary Ajax side created by Rinus Michels on their way to the top. Amid dense fog in Amsterdam's Olympic Stadium, the young Johan Cruyff and Co. hammered the Reds 5–1 and then produced another fine display in a 2–2 draw at Anfield.

The decade ended with Liverpool about to enter a rebuilding period and two forays into the European

Inter-Cities Fairs Cup ended in defeat. In the 1967–68 competition, the classy Hungarians of Ferencvaros became the first continental team to win at Anfield, and the following season the law of averages worked against the Reds after a 2–2 aggregate draw with Athletic Bilbao. As against Cologne, the toss of a coin was required to produce a winner, and this time Ron Yeats's luck deserted him. The Basques went through.

That disappointment emphasised that the road to European success was going to be a long and winding one. But Liverpool were slowly getting there.

5 May 1966
European Cup-Winners' Cup Final

LIVERPOOL 1
BORUSSIA DORTMUND 2

Goals: 0-1 Held (61 mins) 1-1 Hunt (68 mins) 1-2 Libuda (107 mins)

The European Cup-Winners' Cup is the one major trophy that Liverpool have never won – but they went mighty close to landing the prize at the first attempt.

A dramatic final lashed by torrential rain saw the Reds goalless at the interval with Borussia Dortmund, who then took the lead against the second-half run of play. Emmerich's lofted pass floated beyond Smith and Yeats for striker Held to burst between them and lash a shot past Lawrence from 15 yards.

Liverpool regrouped and were level within seven minutes. Thompson collected Smith's pass and raced half the length of the pitch before pulling the ball back for Hunt to score. The Germans claimed the winger had crossed from behind the dead-ball line, but as the pitch markings had been washed away by the rain it was impossible to tell for sure.

However, that was the final piece of fortune to fall Liverpool's way. With only seconds remaining, Hunt's momentary hesitation cost him a clear scoring chance and then a freak goal in extra-time handed Dortmund victory. Lawrence blocked bravely from Held and the ball cannoned clear to Libuda who, although almost 40 yards out, lobbed it straight back towards the empty net.

In the conditions, it could have gone anywhere but it sailed ominously towards the corner of the goal. Yeats raced back in desperate hope of intercepting, but as he arrived on the line, the ball struck the woodwork and rebounded straight at him. Skating across the mud at top speed, he could not avoid it. The ball hit him and bounced cruelly over the line. The cup was lost.

Ian St John battles for possession during the 1966 Cup-Winners' Cup against Borussia Dortmund

The Seventies

Kenny Dalglish scores the goal that beat FC Bruges and won Liverpool the 1978 European Cup

By the start of the 1970s, Liverpool were beginning to get to grips with the demands of European football and the new young team that Shankly had put together began the decade by going all the way to the semi-finals of the Fairs Cup.

In the first round they avenged their defeat by Ferencvaros three years earlier and then made impressive progress to a quarter-final in which an Alun Evans hat-trick saw off a great Bayern Munich side featuring the likes of Franz Beckenbauer, Sepp Maier and Gerd Muller. Liverpool proved that result was no fluke by forcing a 1–1 draw in the Olympic Stadium to set up a last four meeting with Leeds United, only to be edged out by a single goal.

The Reds had gone tantalisingly close to glory yet again, but they would not have long to wait to get their hands on European silverware. Bayern Munich gained a 3–1 aggregate revenge in the following season's Cup-Winners' Cup before Shankly's team started 1972–73 in the UEFA Cup, as the Fairs competition had now been renamed. This time, more German sides in Eintracht Frankfurt and Dynamo Berlin were dismissed by two goal aggregate margins before Dynamo Dresden were beaten both home and away. That set up a semi-final against cup holders Tottenham Hotspur, which was won by Steve Heighway's away goal in a 2–2 aggregate draw.

In the final they faced yet another German team, Borussia Moenchengladbach, and again racked up a healthy lead in the first leg, which was replayed after a downpour washed out the original game. Borussia fought back on their own ground to win the second leg 2–0, but a 3–2 overall scoreline brought the UEFA Cup to Liverpool.

Red Star Belgrade then denied Shankly European Cup success in his final season as boss, and in 1974–75, although Liverpool recorded their biggest continental win in thrashing Norwegian side Stromsgodset 11–0, they could not bring Bob Paisley a debut crown as Ferencvaros beat them again, this time on away goals. But the following term they again lifted the UEFA Cup after having a Ray Clemence penalty save in Dresden to thank for securing their passage into a semi-final with Barcelona. There, a Toshack goal stunned the Nou Camp as Liverpool won the first leg before securing their place in the final with a 1–1 Anfield draw. The Reds faced FC Bruges and had to come from behind to take a 3–2 lead to Belgium, where a 1–1 draw earned them their second European prize.

Winning the League gave Liverpool entry to the European Cup again in 1976–77 and after losing their quarter-final first leg 1–0 in St Etienne they reached the last four on the most thrilling night Anfield has ever seen. Keegan lobbed the Reds level on aggregate inside two minutes but Bathenay restored the visitors' overall lead with a superb long-range strike. Ray Kennedy then scored for Liverpool but they still needed one more goal to go through. Enter "Supersub" David Fairclough to sprint through the French defence with just seven minutes to play and slot home the winner to earn himself a permanent place in Anfield folklore.

The semi-final against FC Zurich was a 6–1 formality and the Reds went on to Rome to beat old adversaries Borussia Moenchengladbach 3–1 in one of the finest of all European Cup finals.

Kevin Keegan had gone to Hamburg by the start of 1977–78 but his replacement, Kenny Dalglish, made sure the European Cup stayed in its new Liverpool home. The Reds beat Benfica home and away before again accounting for Moenchengladbach in the semi-final. They went on to meet FC Bruges in the final, where Dalglish cemented his instant hero status by scoring a sublime winning goal.

However, their reign as champions of Europe ended in the very first round of the 1978–79 competition, when they were drawn against Nottingham Forest in a tie that should really have been the final.

Forest took a 2-0 first leg from which Liverpool could not come back against the eventual cup winners. And the decade ended with a second consecutive first-round exit, this time when an outstanding Dinamo Tbilisi side overturned a 2-1 Anfield defeat with a 3-0 win on their own pitch. The blip, however, would prove to be only temporary.

10 May 1973
UEFA Cup Final, first leg
LIVERPOOL 3
BORUSSIA MOENCHENGLADBACH 0

Goals: 1–0 Keegan (21 mins) 2–0 Keegan (33 mins) 3–0 Lloyd (62 mins)

The first attempt to play this game lasted just 30 minutes as monsoon conditions forced an abandonment. But in that half-hour Shankly saw enough to make the tactical switch that would win the tie.

Spotting Moenchengladbach were weak in the air, he brought in the powerful Toshack to exploit the flaw. He quickly obliged with two headers from which Keegan gave the Reds a 2-0 half-time lead. Keegan was denied a hat-trick by Kleff's penalty save but went on to take the corner that Lloyd headed home to give Liverpool what looked an unassailable lead.

23 May 1973
UEFA Cup Final, second leg
BORUSSIA MOENCHENGLADBACH 2
LIVERPOOL 0

Goals: 1–0 Heynckes (31 mins) 2–0 Heynckes (40 mins)

Moenchengladbach had been given a mountain to climb in the second leg – but they very nearly made it to the summit on a nerve-jangling night for Liverpool.

Although Hughes spooned over the bar in only the fifth minute, it was generally one-way traffic towards the Liverpool goal as the Reds tried to sit on their lead. Rupp missed a sitter and Jensen went close before Callaghan's slip allowed Rupp to cross for Heynckes to score. Worse was to follow as Heynckes curled in a beauty from 20 yards to put his side in touching distance by the interval.

But Liverpool came out for the second half with more purpose and although Moenchengladbach continued to threaten, they began to tire and the Reds held on to bring home their first European trophy.

28 April 1976
UEFA Cup Final, first leg
LIVERPOOL 3
BRUGES 2

Goals: 0–1 Lambert (5 mins) 0–2 Cools (12 mins) 1–2 Kennedy (59 mins) 2–2 Case (61 mins) 3–2 Keegan (pen, 64 mins)

Another tactical managerial masterstroke, this time from Bob Paisley, put Liverpool on course for their second UEFA Cup triumph.

The introduction of substitute Jimmy Case swung the tie the Reds' way as they came back from conceding two goals in the first 12 minutes. First, Neal tried to head a long ball back to Clemence, only for Lambert to nip in and lift it over the goalkeeper. And when a brilliant shot on the turn from Cools made it 2–0 soon after, Liverpool were in deep trouble.

Disjointed throughout the first half, Case's interval arrival transformed the side by allowing Keegan to push further forward. The switch worked as Kennedy scored from the edge of the box and Case levelled with a tap-in after Keegan hit a post. Keegan then added a penalty himself to give Liverpool a slender lead at the final's halfway point

19 May 1976
UEFA Cup Final, second leg
FC BRUGES 1
LIVERPOOL 1

Goals: 1–0 Lambert (11 mins) 1–1 Keegan (15 mins)

Liverpool had stared defeat in the face after just 12 minutes of the final's first leg and by the same point in the return match they were again in a losing position.

But just as they had rallied at Anfield, they did so again in Bruges. Another mistake handed the Belgians an early lead as Smith's touch teed up Lambert from 12 yards. However, the blow only stirred Liverpool into frenzied action and they equalized within four minutes. Hughes rolled a free-kick to Keegan just outside the box and he drove a low shot into Jensen's net.

That deflated Bruges and the Reds' command of the tie grew stronger by the minute. But the Belgians refused to give in and subjected Liverpool to a desperate final few minutes before they could claim their second continental prize.

25 May 1977
European Cup Final

LIVERPOOL 3
BORUSSIA MOENCHENGLADBACH 1

Goals: 1–0 McDermott (28 mins) 1–1 Simonsen (51 mins) 2–1 Smith (65 mins) 3–1 Neal (pen, 83 mins)

When Liverpool at last captured club football's greatest prize, they did so with one of the most complete performances the final has ever seen.

Buoyed by a huge, raucous travelling Kop, the Reds controlled almost the entire first half by pinning the Germans back in their own territory and took the lead within 30 minutes. Callaghan and Heighway broke down the right before the winger's pass inside picked out McDermott galloping through the middle. Taking the ball in his stride, he burst into the box and coolly clipped his shot past Kneib and into the net.

But Borussia responded and enjoyed a spell of mounting pressure either side of half-time that led to a 51st minute equalizer from Simonsen.

Then came the two moments that changed the game. First, with Borussia growing in confidence and menace, Clemence dashed from his line to block superbly at the feet of Stielike. And within ten minutes, Liverpool had struck back with a galvanising second goal. This time it was Smith who was the hero as he headed in Heighway's corner from 15 yards.

That knocked the proverbial stuffing out of Moenchengladbach and the Reds had few further scares before sealing victory with a Phil Neal penalty.

10 May 1978
European Cup Final

LIVERPOOL 1
FC BRUGES 0

Goal: 1–0 Dalglish (65 mins)

In becoming the first British club to win the European Cup twice, Liverpool saw off Bruges with far more comfort than the 1–0 scoreline suggests.

The Belgian champions showed little ambition and relied on an efficient offside trap to frustrate wave after wave of Liverpool attacks. With Souness running the show majestically from midfield, Case was denied twice while Neal and Fairclough were also foiled in a first half of mounting pressure from the Reds.

The pattern continued after the break and the breakthrough eventually came on 65 minutes and proved well worth the wait. Souness split the defence with a brilliantly weighted pass to send Dalglish clear. The striker, showing remarkable cool, dinked the perfect shot over the onrushing Jensen and into the far corner of the goal.

Bruges had a golden opportunity to equalize late on, but Thompson cleared off the line to preserve Liverpool's continental supremacy.

Terry McDermott scores the opening goal of the 1977 European Cup Final against Moenchengladbach

The Eighties

After ending the '70s with two relative failures in Europe, Liverpool wasted little time in making up for those disappointments in the 1980s. After warming up in the 1980–81 Champions Cup with an 11-2 aggregate hammering of Finnish part-timers Oulo Palloseura they beat Aberdeen and then CSKA Sofia, the latter through a stunning Graeme Souness hat-trick. That set up a semi-final against Bayern Munich and another of Liverpool's backs-to-the-wall performances.

A 0–0 draw at Anfield gave the over-confident Germans the advantage, but an injury-hit Reds side performed heroics in Munich to win through thanks to Ray Kennedy's late away goal. The final against Real Madrid proved just as dramatic and although the quality of play did not live up to pre-match expectations, the trophy was won for Liverpool by another late goal, this time scored by Alan Kennedy with just nine minutes left to play.

Anfield had now welcomed the European Cup three times, but while the Reds continued to dominate at home, they crashed out of the next two competitions behind the Iron Curtain. In 1981–-82, CSKA Sofia paid Liverpool back for their 6–1 defeat the previous year by beating them 2–1 on aggregate after extra-time, although a mistake by Bruce Grobbelaar contributed significantly to the defeat. Another gaffe by Grobbelaar saw the Reds lose 2–0 at Widzew Lodz the following season to set up a 3–4 aggregate defeat. However, in 1983–84 the eccentric goalkeeper would redeem himself at the moment when the stakes were highest.

Joe Fagan's first campaign as manager saw Liverpool make majestic progress towards the European Cup final by winning the away leg of every round, including stunning victories in Bilbao, Benfica's famous Stadium of Light and in Bucharest where an outstanding display amid one of the most hostile environments Liverpool had ever experienced clinched a 3–1 aggregate victory. The Reds then faced Roma in the final, which was when Grobbelaar came into his own as a 1–1 draw led to a penalty shoot-out. The moustachioed goalkeeper won the mind game of the gladiatorial spot-kick contest and Liverpool completed a remarkable treble of League Championship, League Cup and European Cup.

Fagan's second and final season in charge should have seen his team retain their trophy as they headed for the final in style, again beating Benfica over two legs and cruising through their semi-final against Panathinaikos 5–0 on aggregate to set up a mouth-watering meeting with Juventus. But what should have been the most triumphant night in Liverpool's continental history turned into the most shameful as rioting spectators wearing the club's colours caused the deaths of 39 Juventus fans when a stadium wall collapsed as a direct result of their mayhem.

For 20 years, Anfield fans had been welcomed across Europe as among the best-natured of all football followers. Now they were held responsible for one of the worst tragedies in the continent's sporting history.

The decrepit, crumbling Heysel Stadium was palpably unfit to host such a high-profile game in the first place, UEFA's ticket allocation policy contributed directly to the initial confrontation that triggered the rioting, the tactics and response to the situation of the Belgian police were completely inadequate, and attacks on Reds supporters by Roma fans the previous year had already created some anti-Italian feeling. But the only fact that matters is that if Liverpool fans had not rampaged across the Heysel terracing and into the ill-fated Sector Z, sending terrified spectators retreating in panic, 39 people who went to Brussels to watch a football match would have returned home alive.

The final went ahead to try and calm the crowd, and Juventus won 1–0. Immediately afterwards, Liverpool withdrew from European competition. UEFA banned both the Reds and all English clubs for an indefinite period. The general exile was ended in 1990, although Liverpool were made to wait a further year for their readmission. They would quickly discover their six years in the wilderness had left them with plenty of catching up to do.

27 May 1981
European Cup Final

LIVERPOOL 1
REAL MADRID 0

Goal: 1–0 A. Kennedy (81 mins)

After loaning out the European Cup to Nottingham Forest for a couple of seasons, Liverpool regained their crown with a goal from a cartoon caveman that sunk the most aristocratic club in football.

Alan Kennedy – nicknamed after Flintstones character Barney Rubble – indulged his habit of scoring vital goals with the most precious strike of his career

Liverpool get their hands on the 1981 European Cup thanks to Alan Kennedy's goal that beat Real Madrid

against Spanish giants Real Madrid. With just seven minutes left and the game goalless, he collected namesake Ray's throw-in on the left, bustled past Cortes's lunge and rifled a rising shot past startled keeper Agustin at his near post.

Kennedy had given early warning of his shooting power with an 11th minute effort that sent Agustin sprawling to save, as Liverpool enjoyed a spell of pressure sandwiched between two threatening passages from Real. With the Spaniards employing a tough man-marking system and showing plenty of movement up front, the match became a battle of tactics and wits. As Camacho curled a shot just wide and Agustin needed two attempts to hold Souness's drive, tension began to mount.

It was almost broken in the opening moments of the second half, when Camacho sprung the Reds' offside trap but chipped both Clemence and the crossbar. The Anfield men immediately regained their composure and as the game headed towards extra-time they grabbed the single goal that had looked increasingly likely to prove decisive. A brilliant save from Agustin prevented Souness from doubling the lead soon after, but the Latin drums had already been silenced by one clubbing blow from Barney Rubble's left boot.

30 May 1984
European Cup Final
ROMA 1
LIVERPOOL 1

Goals: 0–1 Neal (15 mins) 1–1 Pruzzo (44 mins). Penalties: Nicol (missed) 0–0; Di Bartolomei 1–0; Neal 1–1; Conti (missed) 1–1; Souness 1–2; Righetti 2–2; Rush 2–3; Graziani (missed) 2–3; Kennedy 2–4.

While Liverpool's fourth European Cup was won in the individual duel of the final's first-ever penalty shoot-out, the victory was above all one for teamwork and character in the face of adversity.

The Reds had won in their own country in 1978 but here they had to take on Roma in the Italians' home stadium. Liverpool not only emerged as worthy winners but even had the temerity to take an early lead when Johnston's cross was driven into the net by Neal. Liverpool appeared well on top and soon had another "goal" from Souness disallowed for offside. But a game of fluctuating advantage swung Roma's way towards the end of the first half, when Pruzzo equalised with a looping header from Conti's cross.

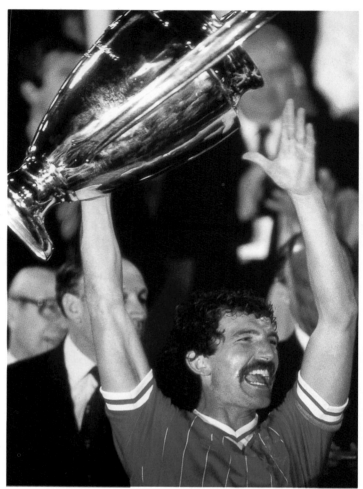

Graeme Souness holds aloft the 1984 European Cup following the penalty shoot-out against Roma

After the break, chances came and went at both ends before fatigue finally ushered in the penalty shoot-out. When Nicol blazed the opener over the bar, Liverpool's cause looked hopeless in the extreme. But suddenly Grobbelaar's eccentricity put his team back in the driving seat.

With Di Bartolomei and Neal both having scored, Conti then skied his effort before successful kicks from Souness, Righetti and Rush made it 3–2 to Liverpool. Up stepped Graziani, whose obviously fraying nerves were further shredded by the sight of Grobbelaar clowning around in front of him, chewing the goal netting and flopping around as if made of rubber. The Italian international poked his shot over the bar, leaving Alan Kennedy with a chance to win the trophy. The only goalscorer of 1981 was an old hand at this sort of thing and, although many of his team-mates could not bear to watch, he thundered his shot into the back of the net to complete another Liverpool mission impossible.

**29 May 1985
European Cup Final**

LIVERPOOL 0
JUVENTUS 1

Goal: 0–1 Platini (pen, 60 mins)

It was supposed to be the night that the European Cup came to Anfield for good. But by the time the Liverpool team walked out in search of the fifth final win that would have given them the trophy for keeps, 39 Juventus fans lay dead and more than 250 were badly injured.

An hour before the scheduled kick-off, fighting broke out between English and Italians sharing the same end of the ground. The drunken violence escalated unchecked and culminated in the Liverpool mob smashing their way through the feeble fencing that seperated the two groups. The fatalities occurred in the ensuing panic when a wall collapsed.

Few of those present on either set of terraces seemed aware of the full scale of the horror and amid an atmosphere dripping with the threat of further bloodshed, it was decided that the game should be played for fear of what might happen if the crowd was simply turned out onto the streets of Brussels.

How the teams found the courage to play out any sort of contest under such appalling circumstances was uncertain but they were worthy of admiration for their part in the efforts to avoid further carnage. The few facts worth recording are that recurrent injuries forced off Lawrenson and Walsh before half-time, and that although Liverpool had the clearer-cut chances, it was Juventus who scored the game's only goal through a Platini penalty after Hansen had brought down Boniek on the edge of the box. But the football was little more than a footnote to the blackest chapter in the otherwise proud history of Liverpool FC and their supporters in Europe.

The Nineties

After six years of European exile, Liverpool took to renewed continental competition with the gusto of a club who knew exactly what they had been missing. Their return to action immediately brought some of the great nights of old back to Anfield once more, but the good times of almost annual trophy-winning triumph steadfastly refused to roll again.

Having been excluded for a year longer than the other English qualifiers, the Reds stepped back into the spotlight in the 1991-92 UEFA Cup and discovered exactly what they were up against as early as round two.

Drawn away at Auxerre, a young Liverpool team in which Jamie Redknapp made his debut was given a footballing lesson. A goal in each half gave the Frenchmen a 2-0 first leg lead and but for Grobbelaar's heroics they would have been out of sight. As it was, the Reds returned to pull off a comeback of St Etienne proportions on another incredible night at Anfield. Liverpool were inspired by the vintage volume of support, Auxerre were terrified by it.

Within four minutes the panicking French side had conceded a penalty in the face of McManaman's twitching run. Molby scored from the spot and the Reds were right back in it. A second goal arrived on the half-hour with the outstanding Mike Marsh's header and when Auxerre defender Frederic Darras was sent off for a second bookable offence, French heads began to drop further still. A Liverpool winner was now seemingly inevitable and duly arrived with just seven minutes to play. Molby's through-ball was converted coolly by Mark Walters to send the Kop into delirium and his team into the last eight.

That was as far as Liverpool went, although the goal that tipped the tie the way of their opponents Genoa was the cruellest of late blows. Amid an electric atmosphere in the Stadio Luigi Ferraris, the Reds dominated the opening stages before a controversial free-kick decision allowed the Italians to take a first-half lead. But with Mike Hooper inspired in goal, it looked like Liverpool would have the narrowest of deficits to overturn back home. Until, that is, two minutes from time, when the referee fell for Ruotolo's dive 35 yards from goal and blew for a foul. Brazilian free-kick expert Branco blasted home an unstoppable shot to give his side a priceless second goal. At Anfield, history could not immediately repeat itself but no one present will ever forget a defeat of truly heroic proportions.

Inspired by a colourful, flag-waving Kop that out-fireworked even the spectacle that had been Genoa, Liverpool bombarded the visitors' goal throughout, only to be denied a superb display from keeper Simone Braglia. Two goals from Uruguayan ace Carlos Aguilera sandwiching a solitary reply from Ian Rush sent Liverpool out of the competition, but they had gone a long way towards restoring their reputation in Europe.

However, instead of constituting a new beginning, the success of that first venture quickly became notable as the exception rather than the rule. After easing past Apollon Limassol in the first round of the 1992-93 Cup-Winners' Cup, Liverpool came unnecessarily unstuck against Spartak Moscow. With six minutes of the first leg left to play in the Russian capital and the scores level at 2-2, Grobbelaar effectively lost the tie by committing a foul in the box for which he was sent off.

He had earlier gifted Spartak their second goal with a poor clearance that was sent straight back over his head and now, with both substitutes already used, his dismissal forced David Burrows to face the resulting spot-kick. He couldn't deny Karpin, and was beaten again soon after as the Muscovites gave themselves a two-goal advantage.

Back at Anfield, the attempt of a young and inexperienced Liverpool side to win through on blood and thunder alone backfired as Spartak looked more confident away from home and finally ran out 2-0 winners after Marsh had been sent off for a heavy challenge.

The Reds still had plenty of ground to make up on the Europeans, and another two-year gap in their continental education – caused this time by rare footballing failures at home – did nothing to help their cause. When they reappeared in the 1995-96 UEFA Cup they began impressively by negotiating a tricky trip to the former Soviet Union outpost of Vladikavkaz through outstanding goals from Redknapp and McManaman. But in round two, after having apparently completed half the job against Brondby by returning from Denmark with a goalless draw, they were caught out and dumped out by a late sucker punch of a goal at Anfield.

In 1996-97, however, the Reds progressed to a Cup-Winners' Cup semi-final against Paris St Germain. But the manner in which they reached the last four, and the fashion in which they left it, offered little evidence to suggest they were any more worldly wise than they had been on their reintroduction to the European game six years earlier.

After a rollercoaster ride against the modest talents of FC Sion, they drew a game they should have won in Bergen before turning in perhaps the most naive and error-strewn performance in the club's long continental history in losing 3-0 in the Parc des Princes. Some measure of pride was restored in a stirring 2-0 Anfield revival, but the real European lessons to be learned lay in the defensive frailties that cost them a final place back in Paris.

Chapter 4

Up for the Cup

Think of Liverpool and you think of European and League domination. But the Reds have also had more than their fair share of cup glory in both domestic cups.

To Bill Shankly, the League Championship was Liverpool's bread and butter, the staple they required and demanded year after year. Cups, he said, were a bonus. And although the Reds have a collection of knockout baubles the envy of almost the entire top flight, it took them far longer to begin raking in those trophies than it did to capture the crown of English champions.

In fact, the FA Cup eluded Liverpool for 73 years, a wait of such proportions that Evertonians delighted in creating a myth that the Liver Birds would take flight from the Liver Building should the Reds ever win the Cup. They did not, of course, although they may have been too elderly to spread their wings by the time Ron Yeats and his colleagues finally paraded the trophy round the city streets before an ecstatic crowd of half a million fans in May 1965. But once their duck was broken, cup triumphs punctuated almost constant success in the League with pleasing regularity.

Liverpool's record in the domestic knockout competitions takes in five FA Cups and five League Cups, the latter matched only by Aston Villa. Yet but for the FA Cup bogey that has hit them so often, it would be better still. The Reds have actually lost more FA Cup finals – six – than they have won, although a record of five wins from their seven League Cup finals has proved handsome compensation.

In fact, Liverpool have been regular record-breakers in the competition, which they initially shunned in its early years. After a controversial final replay defeat by Nottingham Forest in 1978, they went on to lift the trophy for an unprecedented four successive seasons in the early 1980s, as they went unbeaten in 25 ties. The third of those final triumphs, a 2–1 win over Manchester United in 1983, saw Bob Paisley mark his farewell year in charge by becoming the first manager to lift a Wembley trophy after captain Graeme Souness ushered him up the famous 39 steps ahead of the team.

Phil Taylor (left) before the 1950 FA Cup Final

Ian St John's fires home a bullet header against Leeds in extra-time to win the 1965 FA Cup

The Reds also became the first side to win two trophies on the same afternoon at Wembley that day when the League Cup was presented alongside the Milk Cup of the competition's sponsors. The latter trophy now resides permanently in the Anfield trophy room after a replay win over Everton in 1984 saw them collect it for the third year in succession.

Liverpool's biggest final win was the 3–0 FA Cup lesson they gave Newcastle United in 1974, while their largest-ever victory in knockout competition is the 10–0 League Cup thrashing they gave Fulham in 1986. Their highest score in the FA Cup proper is the 8–0 by which they beat Swansea City in a third round replay in 1990, although they had actually gone one better than that score in only their second ever cup tie when they thrashed Newtown 9–0 in an 1892–93 qualifying round, but that was one of the few bright spots in their unremarkable early cup history.

They lost 1–0 to Burnley at the Crystal Palace in the 1914 final through a second-half goal from ex-Everton player Bertie Freeman, but then got no further than the quarter-final until after the Second World War. They reached the final again in 1950 with the team that had won the first post-war Championship three years earlier, but the side was past its peak and lost 2–0 to Arsenal. Many of the players blamed the omission of semi-final hero Bob Paisley for the defeat, as without him they had no one to answer the Gunners' superior physical strength.

Liverpool's reputation as giants in the League meant that their cup bogey exposed them to some of football's greatest shocks, none of which was greater or more ill-timed than the 1988 FA Cup final defeat by Wimbledon. Other infamous humblings at the hands of lower-division sides include those by Peterborough United, Bolton Wanderers and Bristol City in the 1990s, eventually spelling the end of Graeme Souness's managership, and by Worcester City of the Southern League in 1959.

But Liverpool's FA Cup history is also scarred by the tragedy of the Hillsborough disaster in which 96 fans were crushed to death at the 1989 FA Cup semi-final, when a police decision to open an entry gate led to fatal overcrowding on the Leppings Lane terrace. In the aftermath, Kenny Dalglish, the players and their wives earned new respect as the club and its fans grieved together, and when the season eventually resumed they went on to win the Cup by beating Everton on a dramatic and emotional afternoon at Wembley. However, eight years on, the victims' families were still seeking a full inquiry into the events leading up to the disaster, while no one in authority has ever been held responsible for their actions.

Liverpool's domestic cup record

FA Cup		Football League Cup	
Winners	**Runners-up**	**Winners**	**Runners-up**
1964–65	1913–14	1980–81	1977–78
1973–74	1949–50	1981–82	1986–87
1985–86	1970–71	1982–83	
1988–89	1976–77	1983–84	
1991–92	1987–88	1994–95	
	1995–96		

The FA Cup comes to Anfield – at last!

The 1950s were a miserable time for Liverpool in both League and Cup. As they slipped down the First Division in 1953 on their way to relegation the following year, their early dismissal from the FA Cup by Gateshead of the Third Division North was shrouded by a blanket of fog. Six years later, there was no hiding their plight as they crashed out in the third round at

Ron Yeats holds aloft football's most famous trophy and the FA Cup belongs to Liverpool at last following their 1965 victory against Leeds

non-League Worcester City. By the time they next played in the competition they had a new manager – and football's Holy Grail would soon be theirs.

Bill Shankly's first priority was to get Liverpool out of the Second Division, and once he had accomplished that they made instant progress towards both League and Cup success. They reached the FA Cup semi-final in 1962–63, their first season back in the top flight, but lost for the third time that term to a highly-rated Leicester City side.

The Championship occupied Anfield minds the following campaign, but 1964–65 was to be their year at last in the FA Cup. The Reds almost fell victim to a shock of Gateshead or Worcester proportions in the fourth round when they were held to a 1–1 draw at home by Stockport County, who were then bottom of the entire 92-club League pyramid, before winning in a replay. In the quarter-final they again faced Leicester, the only team in the land who appeared to have their measure. This time Liverpool forced a draw at Filbert Street and won the Anfield replay with a goal from that lethal finisher Roger Hunt.

Chelsea proved nowhere near as tough a nut to crack in the semi-final, where goals from Peter Thompson and penalty-taker Willie Stevenson sent Liverpool to Wembley and one of the most famous victories in the club's history.

Although it would be another nine years before Liverpool players would enjoy that taste of victory again, the FA Cup would continue to play a pivotal role in the Liverpool story. The Reds acquitted themselves reasonably well over the next few seasons but then lost the apparent formality of a 1970 quarter-final 1–0 at Watford, who were then lying near the foot of the Second Division. Afterwards, a livid Shankly decided that many of his old warhorses no longer had the stomach for the fight and began building a fresh Anfield dynasty.

The new side he put together reached the final the following season by beating Everton in the semi, but with an average age of just 22 they were beaten 2–1 in extra time by the experience of Arsenal's Double winners. Winger Steve Heighway put Liverpool ahead just two minutes into the supplementary half-hour, but the Gunners scrambled an equalizer before Charlie George fired home the winner.

The area Liverpool had perhaps been found wanting in that match was in goalscoring power up front. But watching from the stands was the solution to the problem – the 19-year-old Kevin Keegan, signed from

Scunthorpe just a few days earlier. Within a year he had struck up an instinctive partnership with fellow newcomer John Toshack, and by 1974 Liverpool were again unstoppable in the FA Cup.

This time they required replays to see off Doncaster Rovers – then 91st in the League – and Second Division Carlisle United before a Toshack winner at Bristol City set up yet another clash with Leicester City. Again, the semi-final finished goalless, but in the replay a dashing second half show capped by goals from Brian Hall, Keegan and Toshack took the Reds back to Wembley.

Liverpool now faced Newcastle United, whose striker Malcolm MacDonald bragged about what he was going to do to the Liverpool defence. In the event, the England striker was denied so much as a sniff of goal by Anfield captain Emlyn Hughes and his 19-year-old centre-back partner Phil Thompson, while at the other end the Reds ran riot. The first half was actually a scrappy affair but a vintage second-half display of passing and movement brought Liverpool a winning margin that has only been bettered five times in more than a century of Cup final football.

Alec Lindsay had a great finish ruled out for offside before Keegan tucked away Tommy Smith's cross for 1–0. When Heighway converted Toshack's flick-on the issue was settled and in the closing stages Shankly began signalling to his players to keep the ball moving as time ran out. They followed his orders but not content merely to retain possession, they built an irresistible 12-pass, seven-man move that swept the length of the field to end with Keegan tapping in the third from another Smith cross. Newcastle, as TV commentator David Coleman put it, were undressed.

Liverpool (0) 2 Leeds United (0) 1 (a.e.t., 0–0 at 90 mins) FA Cup Final, at Wembley Saturday, 1 May 1965

For the players and fans who celebrated Liverpool's famous Wembley win of 1965, victory proved well worth the 75-year wait.

While the Reds' 2–1 extra-time win over an uncompromising Leeds United side was for long periods a grim war of attrition fought out in rain-sodden conditions, it was won by two fine goals scored by a team packed with heroes, the most worthy of whom was defender Gerry Byrne.

Kevin Keegan scores his second goal as Liverpool beat Newcastle 3–0 in the 1974 FA Cup Final

The tough-tackling left-back broke his collar bone when shoulder-charged by Bobby Collins in only the third minute. And with no substitutes allowed Byrne had to battle on, desperately trying to hide his pain from opponents who would mercilessly have targeted any weak link in the Reds' rearguard. Even after the full extent of the injury was diagnosed at half-time, Byrne insisted on continuing once physio Bob Paisley had swathed his upper body in bandages.

When the match finished goalless, the prospect of 30 more minutes play might have finished a lesser man, but not only did Gerry manfully stay the course, he even charged forward to overlap Peter Thompson and swung in a cross that Hunt netted with a stooping header.

Yet Liverpool were soon back to square one as Billy Bremner drove in an excellent equaliser. However, the Reds refused to surrender the initiative and got their reward when Ian Callaghan escaped down the flank. His cross was met by Ian St John, whose diving header won the FA Cup for Liverpool at last.

FA Cup Final 1965

Liverpool:
Lawrence; Lawler, Byrne, Strong, Yeats, Stevenson, Callaghan, Hunt, St John, Smith, Thompson.

Leeds United:
Sprake; Reaney, Bell, Bremner, Charlton, Hunter, Giles, Storrie, Peacock, Collins, Johanneson.

Goals:
1–0 Hunt (93 mins)
1–1 Bremner (101 mins)
2–1 St John (113 mins)

Attendance:
100,000

Referee:
W. Clements
(West Bromwich)

Bob Paisley – and the one that got away

The joy of the 1974 FA Cup Final win was followed by the shock of Bill Shankly's retirement as Liverpool manager. He was succeeded by his right-hand man, Bob Paisley, who went on to become the most successful manager in the history of the British game. But, although the shrewd Geordie filled the Anfield sideboard year after year, the FA Cup jinx that had afflicted the club for so long now denied Paisley a personal set of domestic honours.

The closest his Liverpool teams ever came to landing the game's most famous knockout trophy was in 1977, when they arrived at Wembley as League Champions to face Manchester United in search of the elusive double and – with a European Cup final still to come – the middle leg of an unheard-of treble. However, after a Jimmy Case thunderbolt had instantly equalized Stuart Pearson's soft opener, a cruel deflection wrong-footed Ray Clemence and handed United victory.

Bob Paisley must have felt the FA Cup gods were against him throughout most of his career, as the Reds got no closer to Wembley in the following six years than an epic 1980 semi-final clash with Arsenal that took three replays to decide. A surprise home defeat by Brighton in his final season ensured that Paisley would not break his duck as a manager, with the added irony that the Seagulls' victory was clinched by a trademark drive from ex-Anfield hero Case, although Phil Neal later missed an equalizing penalty chance that would have taken the match to a replay.

Yet, while Liverpool were frustrated in the FA Cup, in the League Cup they could do no wrong. After losing to Southampton in front of only 14,000 in the competition's first year, the Reds had declined to enter until the final was switched to Wembley and a UEFA Cup placed offered to the winners in 1967. Yet even then, they failed to get beyond the fourth round in their first 11 attempts and when they did begin making progress under Paisley, they found their route to glory barred by a familiar foe.

In the late '70s Nottingham Forest were just about the only team in Europe who could match Liverpool at their best, although it took a referee's mistake to hand them victory in the 1978 League Cup Final

20-year-old Ronnie Whelan puts Liverpool ahead in the 1982 League Cup Final against Tottenham

---

FA Cup Final 1982

Liverpool:
Grobbelaar; Neal, Kennedy, Thompson, Whelan, Lawrenson, Dalglish, Lee, Rush, McDermott (Johnson, 75), Souness.

Tottenham Hotspur:
Clemence; Hughton, Miller, Price, Hazard (Villa, 63), Perryman, Ardiles, Archibald, Galvin, Hoddle, Crooks.

Goals:
0–1 Archibald (11 mins)
1–1 Whelan (87 mins)
2–1 Whelan (111 mins)
3–1 Rush (119 mins)

Attendance:
100,000

Referee:
P. Willis
(Co. Durham)

---

replay. After a tense 0–0 draw at Wembley the teams reconvened at Old Trafford, where Forest won by a John Robertson penalty after Phil Thompson was penalized for a tackle on John O'Hare that actually occurred outside the box. Forest also accounted for the Reds in the 1980 semifinal, but Liverpool could not be denied for long.

The following season they reached the final again, where West Ham United snatched a 1–1 draw with a penalty in the last minute of extra time to cancel out Alan Kennedy's opener. The Hammers took the lead in the Villa Park replay, but goals from Dalglish and Hansen brought the trophy back to Anfield.

A young Ian Rush caught the eye in that game, and as he exploded on to the first-division scene properly the following term he was on target when Liverpool retained their cup with a 3–1 comeback win over Spurs. But the hero of that match was two-goal Ronnie Whelan, who proved a match-winner again in 1983 when Manchester United were his victims.

The Old Trafford team took an early lead through Norman Whiteside, but mounting Liverpool pressure led to Alan Kennedy thundering in an equalizer with a quarter of an hour to play. Extra time was required and Whelan, who trained with United as a schoolboy, reminded them what they missed by curling in a sumptuous winner from 20 yards.

By 1984, Paisley had bowed out and been succeeded by Joe Fagan, who carried on where his predecessor left off. That year, Merseyside got the Wembley derby it had waited almost a century for as Liverpool faced Everton in the League Cup Final, although the Reds had taken three games to see off Fulham and required further replays at almost every stage.

The Blues might have taken an early lead when Alan Hansen survived a strong appeal for hand-ball, but a replay was required to decide the contest.

The game was played at Maine Road and was settled midway through the first half by a Graeme Souness piledriver that flew inches above the turf and centimetres inside Neville Southall's left-hand post. The trophy stayed at Anfield, where at the end of the season it was joined by the League Championship and European Cup as Liverpool completed a unique treble.

Liverpool (0) 3 Tottenham Hotspur (1) 1 (a.e.t., 1–1 at 90 mins) League Cup Final, at Wembley Saturday, 13 March 1982

Rarely have the Liverpool virtues of physical fitness and refusal to accept defeat until the final whistle blows been better showcased than in the winning of the 1982 League Cup.

The holders from Anfield found themselves trailing early on to a Steve Archibald goal. Ray Clemence then denied his former team-mates with a string of fine saves, and when Graeme Souness had to clear another Archibald shot off the line near the end, the game looked up for Liverpool.

But then, with just seconds remaining, substitute David Johnson took possession on the edge of the Tottenham box and slipped a short pass inside for Ronnie Whelan to thump home a sensational equalizer.

Spurs were shell-shocked by the goal and slumped to their knees as normal time ended. The Londoners, now drained both physically and emotionally, were on the brink and Bob Paisley pushed them over it with a piece of kidology worthy of Shankly himself. While the men in white lolled on the turf, the Liverpool boss kept his players on their feet, keeping them loose and making them look eager for the extra half-hour.

When play resumed, Spurs could only cling on as best they could as the fitter Reds now rampaged around Wembley's wide open spaces. Something had to give, and with cramp-tortured Tottenham players littering the pitch, a deflected Dalglish cross fell to Whelan. The 20-year-old Dubliner showed a maturity beyond his years to steady himself before making no mistake with what proved to be the decisive finish. A third goal, this time from Rush, scored as Spurs poured forward in desperation, put the icing on the cake for Liverpool.

The Treble Double – so near and yet so far

While the FA Cup eluded both Bob Paisley and Joe Fagan, it took player-manager Kenny Dalglish just one season to get his hands on the famous trophy – but not without first enduring plenty of drama.

Liverpool had rescued themselves twice in the dying minutes of both normal and extra time in the 1985 semi-final thriller against Manchester United, only to lose the replay, and they stared elimination in the face once more exactly 11 months later. This time the Reds trailed Watford 1–0 in a replay with just four minutes to play when Jan Molby saved the day with a penalty that no one wanted to take. Ian Rush added an inevitable winner in extra time and scored the semi-final brace against Southampton that set up the first all-Merseyside FA Cup final.

Everton sought revenge at Wembley for being pipped by their neighbours in the League, but could not deny Liverpool their place in the history books as two goals from Rush and another from Craig Johnston gave the Anfield side a 3–1 win.

The following season, Liverpool made more progress in the League Cup, now under the sponsorship of Littlewoods. After throwing away a place in the 1986 final with two Anfield own-goals that gifted QPR victory, they began their 1986–87 bid by over-

Wimbledon's Dave Beasant dives full stretch to save John Alridge's penalty in the 1988 Cup Final

whelming Fulham 13–2 on aggregate after a 10–0 first-leg romp in which Steve McMahon scored four. They went on to a final meeting with Arsenal, where Rush gave the Reds a first-half lead. But the Gunners hit back to equalize and when Charlie Nicholas's shot was deflected past Grobbelaar, Liverpool's record of never having lost when Rush scored had been broken in the costliest manner possible.

Dalglish's Reds were back at Wembley the following year, and again they were going for the League and Cup double. After storming to the title with some of the most spectacular football the English game has seen, they were white-hot favourites to become the first double double-winners against Wimbledon's self-styled Crazy Gang. Liverpool had looked unstoppable on their way to the final – particularly in dismissing Nottingham Forest from the last four – but at Wembley it all went wrong.

Liverpool looked lethargic, and from the moment referee Brian Hill disallowed a Beardsley goal to award his side a free kick instead, the writing was on the wall. Minutes later Lawrie Sanchez was given a free header to put Wimbledon into the lead before half-time and after the break Liverpool rarely looked like scoring. The referee awarded

Everton 'keeper Bobby Mimms can only watch in desperation as Ian Rush scores to put Liverpool back on level terms in the 1986 FA Cup Final

them a dubious late penalty, but by that point it was almost inevitable that Aldridge would become the first player to have a spot-kick saved in a Wembley final and the double dream had gone.

That was Aldridge's last touch of the match, as he was immediately replaced by Johnston. But 12 months later he would score with his very next FA Cup Final touch – although not before he had thought seriously about quitting the game.

Aldridge's goal came four minutes into the 1989 FA Cup Final against Everton, a match played in the shadow of the semi-final disaster at Hillsborough, in which 96 Liverpool fans were crushed to death against the fencing of the terrace behind Bruce Grobbelaar's goal. The match was abandoned after six minutes and in the aftermath of a heartbreaking succession of funerals, lifelong fan Aldridge was among those who questioned whether he could or should go on. In keeping with the wishes of the victims' families, the competition continued and the Reds reached Wembley with a 3–1 win over Nottingham Forest at a sombre Old Trafford.

The final produced an afternoon of high emotions and drama. Aldridge's opener was cancelled out by McCall seconds before the final whistle, but in extra time Liverpool lifted themselves again and two superb goals from substitute Rush saw them home 3–2. That win set up their third double chance in four years, but the Championship decider six days later would deny them the prize again.

Liverpool (0) 3 Everton (1) 1
FA Cup Final, at Wembley
Saturday, 10 May 1986

Liverpool became only the third team this century to complete the classic League and Cup double when they came from behind to beat their oldest rivals Everton on an action-packed afternoon at Wembley.

The first all-Merseyside FA Cup Final emptied the city as tens of thousands descended on the capital for the historic occasion. Those who gained entry to the packed stadium saw Liverpool settle the better, and although Everton seized the initiative after Lineker put them ahead, the Reds were still in touch at the break. Kenny Dalglish's side levelled when Molby's perfect pass sent Rush through to beat Mimms, but as Everton responded a string of high crosses played havoc with the uncertain-looking Grobbelaar's nerves

A carpet of flowers and scarves turned Anfield into a shrine in the aftermath of the 1989 Hillsborough disaster

and the game looked like slipping away from the Zimbabwean's team.

However, just as suddenly as his flapping had put Liverpool on the rack, a characteristic moment of athletic brilliance galvanised his colleagues into a whirlwind recovery. Just moments after almost coming to blows with team-mate Beglin over yet another mix-up, Grobbelaar offered himself as a back-pass option to the under-pressure Hansen. Instead, the Reds' captain mishit a blind pass across his box and the ball fell for Graeme Sharp to loop a powerful header towards the unguarded net. But from nowhere appeared Grobbelaar to hang like a basketball player at the top of his leap and somehow fingertip the ball over the bar.

That inspired the Reds' defence to dig deep once more and within minutes they took the lead as Rush and Molby combined to give Craig Johnston a tap-in at the back post. There was no looking back, and with Everton stretched by their search for an equalizer, Whelan chipped a long crossfield pass for Rush to volley home and seal the victory. Liverpool had at last won the double.

FA Cup Final 1986

Liverpool:
Grobbelaar; Lawrenson, Beglin, Nicol, Whelan, Hansen, Dalglish, Johnston, Rush, Molby, MacDonald.
Sub not used: McMahon.

Everton:
Mimms; Stevens (Heath, 71), Van den Hauwe, Ratcliffe, Mountfield, Reid, Steven, Lineker, Sharp, Bracewell, Sheedy.

Goals:
0–1 Lineker (28 mins)
1–1 Rush (57 mins)
2–1 Johnston (63 mins)
3–1 Rush (84 mins)

Attendance:
98,000

Referee:
A. Robinson (Portsmouth)

1990–1997 – The ups and downs

The tone of much of what was to follow throughout most of the 1990s was set in the very first FA Cup campaign of the decade, which saw Liverpool veer from the sublime to the ridiculous.

They thrashed Swansea 8–0 with a swashbuckling third-round replay performance and by April were on course for another shot at the double. The Reds went on to land the League but fell in the Cup in a remarkable semi-final. Facing Crystal Palace, Liverpool went ahead through Rush after just 14 minutes before the Eagles began the second half by testing the Reds' defence with a succession of high balls, which caused complete panic in front of Grobbelaar's goal.

Every cross threatened a goal and it wasn't long before two duly arrived. But as full-time approached, Liverpool hit back with two goals in as many minutes from McMahon and penalty-taker Barnes. That appeared to settle the issue, until the Anfield defence failed to deal with yet another hopeful centre and Palace again drew level. A carbon copy of each of their previous goals then won the tie for the Londoners in extra time and began the better part of a decade of footballing vertigo on the part of Liverpool defences.

The following year, the Reds lost in the FA Cup fifth round to Everton in a second replay after the teams had drawn 0–0 at Anfield and then matched each other goal for goal in an astonishing 4–4 draw at Goodison. Although one of the most exciting cup ties ever, that high-scoring game was marked by some more shambolic defending by the Reds, although the chaos on the pitch was soon matched by that off it as Kenny Dalglish resigned as the pressure of the Anfield job took its toll on the Scot.

A new manager, Graeme Souness, brought both success and failure in his first full season in the job. 1991–92 saw Liverpool humbled in the League Cup at lowly Peterborough United before they bounced back to compensate by winning a fifth FA Cup. It wasn't all plain sailing though: in the semi-final, second division Portsmouth were on the verge of pulling off yet another shock before Ronnie Whelan restored order and bundled in a late, late equalizer.

Souness went through the ordeal of watching from the touchline in the knowledge that he needed a triple heart by-pass operation, and went into hospital soon after. Ronnie Moran took charge for the replay, in which Pompey put up equally stubborn opposition and forced Liverpool into becoming the first side to reach Wembley via a penalty shoot-out. In the final itself, Sunderland – also from Division Two – posed Liverpool fewer problems, and goals from Thomas and Rush sealed victory.

After that triumph, though, things began to go badly wrong in Souness's final two years in charge. Liverpool were perhaps unfortunate to make consecutive League Cup fourth round exits at the hands of Crystal Palace and Wimbledon, but the same could not be said of the two FA Cup defeats that eventually forced Souness out.

The Reds had been on the verge of third-round elimination at both Bolton Wanderers and Bristol City in 1993 and 1994 before Rush rescued them with a late goal on each occasion. But as it turned out he merely set up home humiliations, as Liverpool were deservedly beaten by both lower-division sides.

The silver lining of 1993–94 had been the emergence of striker Robbie Fowler, who was given a League Cup debut at Fulham in September, marked it with a goal and went on to score five times in the second leg. And the following term, Fowler's goals took Liverpool back to Wembley in the same competition to give Roy Evans a piece of silverware in his first full season as boss. The young centre-forward scored both goals in the semi-final win over Crystal Palace, but once Wembley was reached it was Steve McManaman who emerged as the hero of a 2–1 win over Bolton.

Fowler was in the goals again two years later and went into the final against Manchester United looking to become the first player to score in every round since

Ian Rush sinks Everton in the 1989 FA Cup Final

Chelsea's Peter Osgood in 1970. But in a match as dull as Liverpool's much-criticised white team suits were flashy, he received scant service and could only watch as David James's clearance punch deflected off Rush for Cantona to volley a late winner through a crowd of Liverpool players.

And the chance to make up for that disappointing show was delayed for at least another year in 1996–97, as two defensive shockers put the Reds out of both knockout competitions, their League Cup run ending at Middlesbrough and a two-goal lead being meekly surrendered in a 4–2 FA Cup defeat at Chelsea. This time no one could blame the suits.

Liverpool (0) 2 Sunderland (0) 0
FA Cup Final, at Wembley
Saturday, 9 May 1992

FA Cup Final 1992

Liverpool:
Grobbelaar; Jones, Wright, Burrows, Nicol, Houghton, Thomas, Molby, McManaman, Saunders, I. Rush.
Subs not used: Walters, Marsh.

Sunderland:
Norman; Owers, Bennett, Ball, Rogan, D. Rush (Hardyman, 68), Atkinson, Bracewell, Armstrong (Hawke, 77), Byrne, Davenport.

Goals:
1–0 Thomas (47 mins)
2–0 Rush (67 mins)
Attendance:
79,554
Referee:
P. Don
(Middlesex)
Booking: Burrows (foul)

Ian Rush's 1992 goal against Sunderland made him the record scorer in FA Cup finals

There was a certain irony in the fact that the trophy won to mark Liverpool's centenary year should be the one that had eluded them for the better part of their existence.

The initial exchanges suggested that manager Souness, watching just days after leaving hospital following heart surgery, would suffer few scares as Liverpool opened up Sunderland's defence, only for Thomas to spoon his shot over the bar. Rush then tested the Wearsiders' goalkeeper Norman, but as the half wore on, the second-division side began to create some chances of their own.

Grobbelaar did well to scramble a save from Ball at his near post and Wright deflected a drive from Bracewell wide of the target. Striker Byrne then squandered two more chances before McManaman showed his class with a mazy run that should have won the Reds a 44th-minute penalty but referee Philip Don ignored Bracewell's trip in the box.

With John Barnes missing the final through injury, it was left to the young and precocious talent of Steve McManaman to provide flair which he duly did to great effect. It took just two minutes for the 20-year-old to create Liverpool's opener as he burst past Atkinson and took three defenders out of the game with a superb pass that Thomas hooked into the net from 12 yards.

The McManaman-inspired Reds now dominated, and after Saunders headed against the bar Thomas fed Rush inside the box and the master striker calmly swept home a record fifth goal in FA Cup finals. Liverpool had ridden their luck at times on their way to Wembley, but their trophy-winning habit had not deserted them.

Chapter 5

The Premiership Stars

Big names and big money have made the English League the best in the world. Here are some of the players who have spearheaded Liverpool's title challenges

All statistics correct to the start of 1997–98 season

Phil **Babb**

RECORD transfer fees are normally paid out for strikers rather than defenders, and three years after Liverpool broke the bank to land centre-back Phil Babb the jury was still out on whether the investment was money well spent.

Babb made his name with the Republic of Ireland at the 1994 World Cup and went straight into the Liverpool line-up after his move from Coventry the following September, to play on the left of a back three. The former winger's electric pace and powers of anticipation meant he looked ideally suited to the role, while he was also useful in the air – another area in which the Reds had been struggling.

The former Millwall and Bradford player quickly became an automatic selection, and after being nearly ever-present in his first season was a regular for the bulk of the 1995–96 campaign before being sidelined by a bruised toe in March. He returned in time to claim an FA Cup Final place and played throughout

Babb was bought from Coventry for £3.75 million

Phil BABB

Born:
30 November 1970
Birthplace:
Lambeth, London
Height:
6ft
Weight:
12st 3lb
Position:
Defender
Games:
128
Goals:
1
Previous clubs:
Coventry City,
Bradford City,
Millwall
Transfer fee:
£3.75 million
International status:
Republic of Ireland
international

the following term, until being ruled out first by suspension and then by a cartilage operation early in 1997, after which he failed to regain his place.

For while Babb had always impressed with his recovery tackling and helped Liverpool return to trophy-winning ways, he looked uncomfortable in a three-man defence when dragged wide to cover behind the left wing-back. Although he had scored 10 times in his first 34 matches for Bradford City – for whom he operated occasionally as a striker – it took him 89 games to get off the mark with the Reds, perhaps as a result of the attention he was required to pay to his defensive duties.

It may be no coincidence that Babb enjoyed the best form of his career when operating as one of a pair of centre-backs during Ireland's 1994 World Cup campaign. A chance in the flat back-four to which Liverpool reverted during the closing stages of 1996–97 might have been the key to scaling those dizzy heights once more.

John **Barnes**

THE Liverpool career of John Barnes has been written off more often than the cartoon rolling-stock of Wacky Races. But every time the football obituarists report his imminent demise, he has a remarkable habit of making them eat their words.

Barnes was at his majestic peak in the first half of his Anfield career, when he was twice Footballer of the Year as his unstoppable wing play steered Liverpool to the Championship in 1987–88 and 1989–90. However, in the early 1990s, with the approach of his 30th birthday, he was struck by the first serious injuries of his career, the worst of which ruled him out of the start of the first Premier League season. Having failed a fitness test before the 1992 FA Cup Final, he

John Barnes switched from left wing to centre midfield in the latter part of his Anfield career

headed for that summer's European Championships, only to rupture an Achilles tendon in England's final warm-up game. Sidelined for almost six months, he lost pace and gained weight, and another missed pre-season the following year saw him being criticised as a shadow of his former self.

But then in 1994–95 Barnes reinvented himself as a central midfielder, pulling the strings from deep while younger legs did his running for him. Extra fitness work during the summer lessened the effects of advancing age, and the next term he missed just three games, scored his 100th Liverpool goal and captained the Reds at Wembley.

Yet he was unable to lift any silverware as skipper, and 1996–97 dawned with the arrival of Patrik Berger, once again apparently spelling

John BARNES

Born:
7 November 1963
Birthplace:
Kingston, Jamaica
Height:
5ft 11in
Weight:
12st 7lb
Position:
Midfielder
Games:
404
Goals:
107
Previous club:
Watford
Transfer fee:
£900,000
International status:
England international

the end for Barnes. This time he reacted by scoring on the opening day, and missed just two games before being dropped for the first time in his Anfield life as Liverpool went for all-out attack at the season's end. That omission hurt Barnes and over the summer of 197, with the arrival of Paul Ince, it became painfully obvious that he was surplus to requirements. In August, therefore, Barnes ended a 10 year association with the Reds and joined Newcastle on a free transfer

Stan Collymore

WHEN Roy Evans paid Nottingham Forest a British record £8.5 million for Stan Collymore in the summer of 1995, he and the whole of football knew he was taking a gamble on a talented but temperamental striker who had never lasted more than two years at any of his former clubs. The leopard failed to change his spots and two seasons later Evans decided to cut his losses and sold the misfit to Aston Villa for £7 million.

Few players have endured a more turbulent or frustrating Anfield career than Collymore. Fined for criticising the club in print, failing to turn up for a reserve-team game and for regularly missing training, the tall striker was also at the centre of a row over his refusal to move to Merseyside from his Midlands home. But while few Liverpool players have caused as much trouble, few have also had as much raw talent.

Stan Collymore had the talent but, crucially, not the consistency to succeed at Anfield

That is why, despite his difficulties, Collymore was always a huge favourite with the Anfield faithful, who willed him to succeed just as much as did the manager who bought him and believed he had the potential to match Brazilian ace Ronaldo, the finest player in the world game.

Fast and powerful, the big centre-forward looked the perfect foil for Robbie Fowler and someone who could add even more variety to the Reds' already potent attack. But, despite scoring a debut winner, his early inability to comprehend Liverpool' s passing game reduced him to little more than a spectator. Then at the end of 1995, he and Fowler suddenly clicked.

Stan COLLYMORE	
Born:	22 January 1971
Birthplace:	Stone, Staffordshire
Height:	6ft 2in
Weight:	13st 11 lb
Position:	Striker
Games:	81
Goals:	35
Previous clubs:	Nottingham Forest, Southend United, Crystal Palace, Stafford Rangers, Walsall, Wolverhampton Wanderers
Transfer fee:	£8.5 million
International status:	England international

Dropping deep and roving out to the flanks, Collymore created a hat-trick for his striking partner against Arsenal, destroyed his old club NottinghamForest single-handedly and went on to help the Reds' strike-force become the most productive in the Premiership.

However, the old problems rather than the new form surfaced in 1996–97 and after being in and out of the side, he was sold at the season's end. Collymore believed his 34 goals from 69 starts meant he did not fail at Liverpool. Anfield' s empty trophy cabinet from the period said otherwise.

Robbie Fowler

ROBBIE Fowler is a young man in a hurry.

He scored on his senior debut as an 18-year-old in the League Cup at Fulham, and followed up in the Anfield return by becoming the first Liverpool player to score five times in a game since Ian Rush achieved the feat a decade earlier. Fowler opened his league account at only the third time of asking, and fired his first Premiership hat-trick just two matches later. He began his first full season by netting the fastest hat-trick in Premiership history and ended by breaking the 30 goals barrier and picking up a League Cup-winners' medal. 1995–96 saw Fowler omitted from the first two starting line-ups over some pre-season slacking, but he bounced back to score on his return at Spurs, push Alan Shearer all the way for the title of England's leading goalscorer, put four past Bolton on his way to another best-ever total of 35 goals from 53 games, and see only an FA Cup Final blank prevent him from becoming the first player to score in every round since Peter Osgood in 1970.

Fowler went on to score his first international goal the following term, and another four against a luckless Middlesbrough in December 1996 saw him reach the milestone of 100 goals for Liverpool in 165 games – one fewer than Rush took. He finished the season with 31 goals, and might have topped his previous best had he not missed five appearances through injury and been ruled out of the campaign's last three games by an unfortunate send-ing-off at Everton.

Although smaller and squatter than his mentor Rush, Fowler shared the master's deadliness inside the penalty box but also demonstrated an ability to

Robbie Fowler exploded onto the Premiership scene as a teenager, but played with the skill and confidence of a seasoned League campaigner

score spectacularly from a distance as well. Blessed with the quickest of feet and an uncanny ability to arrive in the right place at the right time, he quickly added much of Rush's workrate to his game, emerging as the most promising striker of his generation. At the time they were set, the records of Roger Hunt and Ian Rush were expected never to be broken. At just 22, Robbie Fowler already looked the man to eclipse them all.

Robbie FOWLER

Born:
9 April, 1975
Birthplace:
Liverpool
Height:
5 ft 11 in
Weight:
11st 10lb
Position:
Striker
Games:
188
Goals:
127
Previous clubs:
None
Transfer fee:
None
International status:
England international

Bruce **Grobbelaar**

BRUCE Grobbelaar's initial eccentricities often looked likely to bring his Liverpool career to a swift end in the early '80s. It is a tribute to his goalkeeping ability rather than his showmanship that he stood between the Anfield posts until he was nearly 37. And even then the colourful Zimbabwean was moved on in order to speed up the development of the young David James, rather than because of any terminal waning of his footballing powers.

Grobbelaar was at his peak during the mid- to late-'80s, when his contribution to the European Cup and double successes of that period made up for the mistakes of his initial impetuosity. But even as late as the start of the Premiership era he was still one of the best shot-stoppers in the game, and was as determined as ever to keep his place in the side. An attack of

Bruce GROBBELAAR

Born:
6 October 1957
Birthplace:
Durban, South Africa
Height:
6ft 1in
Weight:
13st
Position:
Goalkeeper
Games:
610
Goals:
None
Previous clubs:
Vancouver Whitecaps
Transfer fee:
£250,000
International status:
Zimbabwe international

Bruce Grobbelaar marshalls his defence in 1994

meningitis had sidelined him for four months during 1988–89, and after handing in a transfer request, on not being granted an instant recall once recovered, he proved his point by keeping 11 clean sheets in 21 games when he did get back in. And while he continued to drop the odd clanger, a superb performance against Manchester United in January 1994 showed he was still capable of instinctive brilliance.

However, after being ever-present for five consecutive League campaigns, he began to become more susceptible to injury in his final years. A damaged hand cost him a few games in 1991, while hamstring strains suffered against Leeds United in 1992 and 1994 respectively threatened his FA Cup Final place and then marked the final curtain-call of his Anfield career. He may have departed with a wimper not a bang, but his spirit and goalkeeping could never be described in the same terms.

Steve **Harkness**

DETERMINATION and aggression are the qualities that characterise Steve Harkness's game – but patience is the virtue he has needed most in his eight years at Anfield.

Signed as an 18-year-old by Kenny Dalglish after making just 13 appearances for Carlisle United, he had to wait for his chance at Liverpool. Seen as a hard-working midfielder by his first club, Harkness was at home anywhere on the left flank and even played for a spell as a striker in the Reds' reserve team. And even though it is as a defender that he has since made his mark, he still has a keen eye for goal, as trademark blasts from a distance proved against Bolton and Manchester City in 1995–96.

That was the first Anfield season in which

Harkness enjoyed a long run in the team, seizing his chance at left wing-back after Stig Inge Bjornebye broke his leg towards the end of the previous term. Although not the quickest of players, his stamina, commitment and tough tackling made him a useful performer in the role. But he really came into his own when switched to centre-back, where he helped end a dreadful run of form that had plagued the team in November 1995. A Liverpool side hit by injuries and international calls relied on fire and physical courage to get back to winning ways on a numbingly cold day at Bolton, and it was the outstanding Harkness who superbly marshalled the more experienced forces around him.

However, it wasn't long before he found himself playing the waiting game once more, after suspension cost him his place early in the New Year. And when he got another chance, in April 1996, he suffered a broken leg at Coventry in only his second game

back. That injury put him out of the game for more than a year, but it is a measure of the esteem in which he is held at Anfield that he was offered a new contract before he was even out of plaster.

David **James**

DAVID James is a player more familiar than most with football's habit of knocking you down at the very moment you feel on top of the world.

Having followed up a £1 million move to Liverpool in 1992 by going straight into the first team, a fragile defence then helped him concede 20 goals in his first 11 matches before he was eventually left out of the team for his own protection. He got another chance at that season's end, but his confidence remained scarred by that debut experience and it took the departure of Bruce Grobbelaar and a public assurance from Roy Evans that he was now Anfield's Number One to chase away the shadow of his illustrious predecessor.

Working with goalkeeping coach Joe Corrigan, James improved almost by the week until he was universally acclaimed as the most promising young 'keeper in England. Hugely-tall but remarkably quick and agile for such a big man, James displayed his excellent spring and agility to become one of the top shot-stoppers in the Premiership. And although following in the eccentric footsteps of most members of

Steve HARKNESS

Born:
27 August 1971
Birthplace:
Carlisle
Height:
5ft 10in
Weight:
11st 2lb
Position:
Defender
Games:
96
Goals:
4
Previous club:
Carlisle United
Transfer fee:
£75,000
International status:
England youth international

David James demonstrates the accurate distribution that has triggered many a dangerous Liverpool attack and led to an England call-up in 1997

David JAMES

Born:
1 August 1970
Birthplace:
Welwyn, Hertfordshire
Height:
6ft 5in
Weight:
14st 2lb
Position:
Goalkeeper
Games:
207
Goals:
None
Previous club:
Watford
Transfer fee:
£1 million
International status:
England international

the goalkeepers' union by dying his hair in varying colours, he became increasingly authoritative and confident on the pitch.

His rise culminated in his first England cap in 1997, against Mexico only for Dame Fortune to throw a spanner in the works once more. James was criticised for showing nerves on his international debut, and then went on to gift opponents a string of vital goals through concentration lapses that helped sink Liverpool's Championship challenge on the run-in. He was forced to shoulder more than his share of blame for that failure, but could take heart from the fact that for all but the final weeks of the season he had been consistently the best 'keeper in the land.

Rob Jones

ROB Jones enjoyed a meteoric rise to the top of his profession, only to see his burgeoning career frustratingly stalled by injury.

Signed at 19, after impressing Graeme Souness in a game the Reds' boss had attended with the intention of checking on a different player entirely, he made an instant debut at Manchester United, was an England international within 20 matches and ended his first season with an FA Cup-winners' medal. The boyhood Liverpool fan, whose grandfather Bill was one of Anfield's 1946–47 title winners, went on to cement his reputation as the best right-back in the country, only to fall victim to misfortunes of selection and injury. Quick enough to outpace even the fastest of wingers, confident on the ball and among the finest timers of a tackle around, Jones was an automatic choice when fit, although a succession of niggling knocks and a susceptibility to illness prevented him from becoming a perennial fixture in the line-up.

When Roy Evans introduced a wing-back system in 1994, the Wrexham-born defender

The pace and skill of Rob Jones rapidly established him as a highly talented right-back

Rob JONES	
Born:	5 November 1971
Birthplace:	Wrexham, Clwyd
Height:	5ft 8in
Weight:	11st
Position:	Defender
Games:	214
Goals:	None
Previous club:	Crewe Alexandra
Transfer fee:	£300,000
International status:	England international

used his pace to good effect in getting up and down the right flank, and his precise crossing created plenty of chances for his strikers. But long-term injury to left wing-back Stig Inge Bjornebye, and the arrival of the right-sided Jason McAteer from Bolton Wanderers in 1995–96, saw Jones switched to the opposite side of the pitch. He performed creditably in the role but often looked ill at ease there, as the need to cut inside on to his favoured right foot limited the supply of crosses from the bye-line.

Furthermore, a lack of opportunity to impress at right-back cost him his England place first won in 1992 before injury was finally added to insult. A fractured vertebra, diagnosed after the 1996 FA Cup final, forced him to rest for almost six months; and on his return to fitness he found himself frozen out of the side. Given his earlier excellence, at the start of the 1997–98 campaign the challenge was as much for the management to find a place for him as it was for him to break back into the team.

Jason **McAteer**

JASON McAteer earned his dream move to Liverpool with a series of all-action performances at the heart of the Bolton Wanderers midfield. But his switch to Anfield was followed by another transformation that made him one of the finest wing-backs in the country.

The boyhood Kopite first caught the eye playing on the right of Ireland's midfield during the 1994 World Cup, but Roy Evans had to wait another year before eventually getting his man. Signed in September 1995, McAteer was given his first chances in his accustomed central berth before a shrewd tactical switch three months later saw him really hit top gear. For the visit of Manchester United, Evans switched Rob Jones to the left wing-back slot to allow the new boy to take over on the right. He more than justified that selection in a 2–0 win, and went on to make the position his own over the next season and a half.

McAteer's energy, natural fitness and attacking instincts made him ideal for the role and he quickly proved a prime source of scoring chances with his crossing from the flank. Although he lacked the true winger's predilection for crossing from the bye-line at pace, the former Marine part-timer covered more ground along the touchline than almost any other member of the team.

Being anchored to the flank staunched the supply of goals he had provided from midfield at Bolton, but in first subduing David Ginola and then going on to set up Liverpool's vital third goal in the thrilling 4–3 win over Newcastle in April 1996, he showed he was just as valuable in other areas. McAteer missed just one game of the 1996–97 campaign at wing-back, but showed at international level that he is still more than useful in the centre of the park. However, in his first two terms at Liverpool he looked a far better prospect shuttling up and down the line than fighting it out in the heat of the midfield battle.

Jason McATEER

Born:
18 June 1971
Birthplace:
Birkenhead
Height:
5ft 11in
Weight:
11st 10lb
Position:
Midfielder
Games:
91
Goals:
4
Previous club:
Bolton Wanderers
Transfer fee:
£4.5 million
International status:
Republic of Ireland international

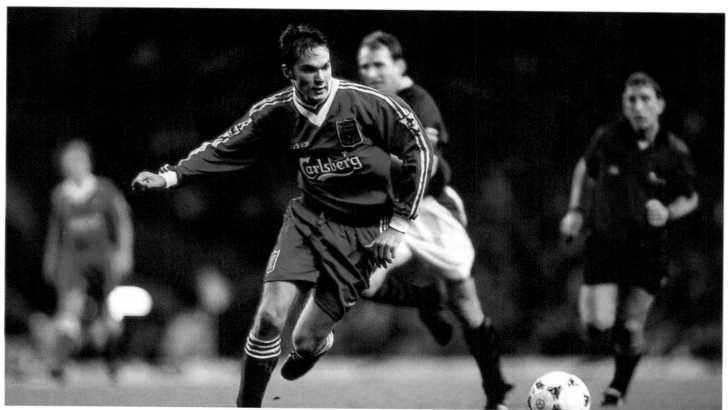

Jason McAteer shows typical determination to break forward during the 1995 derby match at Anfield

Steve **McManaman**

STEVE McManaman was the first product of Liverpool's modern youth system to break through into the big time. And he did it so impressively that by 23 he was a full England international and had both winners' medals and Man of the Match awards from League and FA Cup finals.

The skinny youngster was thrown into the side as a right winger at the start of the 1991–92 season, and immediately impressed with his speed, skill and trickery. But McManaman had never considered himself a winger in the traditional sense; and when he was handed a free role in Roy Evans's new-look formation of 1994, he quickly matured into the most dangerous attacker in English football with his intelligence, awareness and tactical appreciation. However, McManaman remained more of a creator than a taker of chances himself, marring his peerless approach play with weak finishing. But with his friend Robbie Fowler leading the Liverpool attack, the fleet-footed midfielder could afford to set up chances for others rather than himself, which was what he did best.

After starring for England in the 1996 European Championships, the one thing that appeared to pose any sort of threat to his continuing rise was the demand placed on his talents by his brilliance with both club and country. Even though he had the stamina to be a top-class distance runner, a schedule of 90 matches in his first two senior seasons naturally took its toll on such a young campaigner. By the end of 1996–97, he had missed just three of the 159 games the Reds had played in three seasons, not including a further 20-odd internationals. A long-standing knee problem required a summer of rest which ruled him out of another tour of England duty. In the long term player, club and country may turn out to be grateful for that refreshing break.

Steve McManaman was Liverpool's most dangerous attacking force throughout the early 1990s

Steve McMANAMAN	
Born:	11 February 1972
Birthplace:	Liverpool
Height:	6ft
Weight:	10st 6lb
Position:	Midfielder
Games:	283
Goals:	47
Previous clubs:	None
Transfer fee:	None
International status:	England international

Dominic **Matteo**

WHILE Robbie Fowler and Steve McManaman rocketed to soccer stardom as precocious youngsters, their fellow-graduate of the Liverpool School of Excellence, Dominic Matteo, has taken a slower but no less certain route to the top.

Having joined the team which he grew up supporting in Southport from the age of ten, in his teens he was marked down by the club as a late developer, despite having played for England at Youth and Under-21 level. At 19 he was given a debut at Manchester City on the left of midfield, but appeared lacking in confidence and failed to make a lasting impression in that or any of the other 10 games he played in 1993–94. However, when he returned to the first team three years later he seemed finally to have come of age as a Premiership performer.

Injuries at the start of the 1996–97 campaign handed him his favoured role at the heart of a three-man defence, where he performed so well that within two months he found himself in the full England squad and being compared favourably to Liverpool legend Alan Hansen.

Hansen himself declared that Matteo was "a better player than I was at 22", and the aptitude the youngster showed for bringing the ball out of defence meant the comparison was anything but far-fetched. Calm and comfortable in possession, the long-striding defender's excursions into midfield provided his team with another potent attacking threat, never better illustrated than in the 5–1 Anfield rout of Chelsea in September 1996 when he dribbled from box to box before sending Patrik Berger in to score.

A tall and rangy defender, Matteo compensated for what he lacked in physical strength with excellent timing, pace and decision-making, and looked comfortable in any of the three centre-back slots. As a comparative novice in 1996–97, he made the occasional mistake but learned quickly from them: and by the season's end looked ready to compete for a regular place in years to come.

Jan **Molby**

NOT many League and FA Cup double-winners consider themselves under-achievers. But then not many of them are as talented as Jan Molby, arguably the most skilful player ever to represent the Reds.

The big Dane was one of the finest players of his generation, but a vicious circle of injury and weight problems cost him huge chunks of an 11-year Liverpool career in which he won just four major medals and played only around 200 games. Bought as a replacement for Graeme Souness in 1984, he made

Dominic MATTEO	
Born:	24 April 1974
Birthplace:	Dumfries
Height:	6ft 1in
Weight:	11st 10lb
Position:	Defender
Games:	65
Goals:	None
Previous clubs:	None
Transfer fee:	None
International status:	England Under-21 international

Dominic Matteo impressed all with his control

more than 100 appearances in his first three seasons and was second-highest scorer in the double-winning campaign of 1985–86.

Molby's passing, close control and cannonball shot alone justified the price of admission to Anfield throughout his time with the Reds, but after breaking a foot during the 1987–88 pre-season his appearances became fewer and farther between, particularly in the 1990s during the Premiership years, in which he never started more than a dozen league games in any season. Part of the problem was the lack of a full-time physiotherapist, before the appointment of Mark Leather in 1994, since in his desperation to play the unsupervised Molby often tried to make an early comeback before he was either fully recovered or match-fit, thereby inevitably exposing him-

Jan MOLBY	
Born:	4 July 1963
Birthplace:	Kolding, Denmark
Height:	6ft 1in
Weight:	14st 7lb
Position:	Midfielder
Games:	280
Goals:	58
Previous clubs:	Ajax Amsterdam, Kolding IF
Transfer fee:	£575,000
International status:	Denmark international

self to further damage.

He began the 1994–95 season in vintage form by orchestrating a 6–1 rout of Crystal Palace, but 11 games later his injury jinx struck again. Molby managed just three more appearances that term, and by December 1996 had accepted the player-manager's job at Swansea City. He left the Liverpool fans with fewer memories than he might have done, but enough of the highest quality to ensure that he will always be remembered as a true Anfield great.

Steve **Nicol**

OVER 13 years at Anfield, Steve Nicol proved himself one of the most reliable and versatile of all Liverpool players. He arrived as a 19-year-old right-back in 1981, went on to become 1989 Football Writers' Player of the Year as a left-back, played in every outfield position for the Reds and was still holding down a centre-back spot when well into his 30s.

Nicol was initially taken under the wing of fellow-Scots Dalglish, Souness and Hansen, and although he was invariably the butt of their practical jokes he soon proved worthy of their company on the field as well as off it. After breaking into the team on the right of midfield and scoring in the Merseyside derby at 21, he became a European Cup-winner a year later despite missing a penalty in the final shoot-out.

Having replaced Phil Neal at right-back in the 1985–86 double-winning team, he then switched to the opposite flank to enjoy one of his greatest moments – a superb televised hat-trick at Newcastle in September 1987. That demonstrated the shooting prowess Nicol could add to his other qualities of speed, skill, stamina, tough tackling and an aerial ability surprising for a comparatively small player.

His apparent invulnerability to injury made him even more valuable to the club, particularly

Steve NICOL

Born:
11 December 1961
Birthplace:
Irvine, Scotland
Height:
5ft 10in
Weight:
12st
Position:
Defender
Games:
453
Goals:
43
Previous club:
Ayr United
Transfer fee:
£300,000
International status:
Scotland international

during the Souness years when his experience became vital as many senior players spent more time in the treatment room than on the pitch. The end only came for Nicol when Roy Evans revamped his defence in 1994 and the long-serving Scot was forced to bow to younger signings John Scales and Phil Babb. He took up a player-coach' s role at Notts County early in 1995, but it was a measure of his enduring quality that he was back facing Liverpool in the Premiership at the heart of Sheffield Wednesday' s defence a full two years later.

Jamie **Redknapp**

FOR most footballers, representing their country is a dream come true. For Jamie Redknapp, however, it quickly became a nightmare as three brief England appearances cost him more than a year out of the game through injury.

A precocious enough talent for Kenny Dalglish to pay £350,000 for him as a 17-year-old in 1991, Redknapp went on to make a scoring league debut before the year was out and become a regular in midfield during 1992–93. Being thrown into a side which, under Graeme Souness, was regularly in crisis made his baptism tougher than many Liverpool starlets had faced in the past; and while Redknapp' s precise passing meant he rarely gave away possession, the great expectations surrounding him meant he was sometimes accused of not being positive enough.

As stability returned to Anfield in the mid-90s, Redknapp began to exert a greater influence on the course of matches, opening up defences with perceptive, play-switching passes to free the likes of Fowler and McManaman ahead of him and showing a greater willingness to use his own piledriver of a shot.

But just as his career looked ready to take off with both club and country, things went painfully awry. After beginning the 1995–96 campaign in the best form of his life, a torn hamstring suffered on England duty kept him out for four months. He returned in time to make the national Euro '96 squad, but after coming on as a substitute to turn the game against Scotland he was stretchered off before the end with damaged ankle ligaments, effectively costing him the entire first half of the 1996–97 campaign. Once back to

Just as Jamie Redknapp was maturing into a top-class midfielder he was struck down by injury

Jamie REDKNAPP

Born:
25 June 1973
Birthplace:
Barton-on-Sea
Height:
6ft
Weight:
12st 10lb
Position:
Midfielder
Games:
209
Goals:
21
Previous clubs:
Bournemouth,
Tottenham Hotspur
Transfer fee:
£350,000
International status:
England international

health, he ended that season by turning out for England in a friendly against South Africa – and breaking his ankle before half-time, thereby waving goodbye to another four months of the 1997–98 season. Both Liverpool and England missed him as much as he missed them.

Neil **Ruddock**

NEIL Ruddock's Anfield career has gone through more highs and lows than a manic depressive on a mountaineering holiday.

Bought by Graeme Souness at the start of the 1993–94 season, the central defensive partnership he first formed with Mark Wright proved solid enough in the air and the tackle but was vulnerable to pace on the ground, although Ruddock had played his first games with Millwall as a speedy winger. However, a change of tactics under Roy Evans to incorporate a three-man central defence provided Ruddock with the protection he needed to produce the best form of his time at Anfield, as Liverpool won the League Cup.

His aggression and sleeves-up commitment, as much as his cheeky character and rolling-down of Eric Cantona's trademark upturned collar, made "Razor" a cult hero of the fans and, while he was as determined as ever in defence, the extra support he now received allowed him to unleash his accurate left foot more often and trigger attacks with his precise long-range passing. The move that led to Liverpool's goal of the 1996–97 season – scored by Robbie Fowler in Bergen – was set up by Ruddock's long pass out of defence.

Having largely curbed the disciplinary problems which had earned him a reputation in his early days, and reduced the regularity of his appearances in the tabloids, the main battle Ruddock then had to face with the Reds was against his own waistline as he displayed

Neil RUDDOCK	
Born:	9 May 1968
Birthplace:	Wandsworth, London
Height:	6ft 2in
Weight:	12st 12lb
Position:	Defender
Games:	149
Goals:	12
Previous clubs:	Tottenham Hotspur, Southampton, Millwall, Tottenham Hotspur, Millwall
Transfer fee:	£2.5 million
International status:	England international

Neil Ruddock's determination and commitment made him a big favourite with the Liverpool fans

a tendency to pile on the pounds during spells of inactivity. Those spells became disappointingly long during 1996–97 as his appearance in fewer than half the Reds' games saw him pondering a transfer request. But a return to the side after Evans switched his formation to 4-4-2 in the closing weeks of the season left him in good heart for the 1997–98 campaign.

Ian **Rush**

WHILE the Premiership years saw Ian Rush's Anfield career enter its twilight years, he still had plenty to offer the Reds, not least in guiding the ascent of his shooting-star successor Robbie Fowler.

The record goalscorer's position as Liverpool's elder statesman was confirmed by his appointment as club captain in 1993, and he proved a fine leader by example to the young team around him, lifting the League Cup at Wembley in 1995. He was not scoring as freely as in his earlier years but was every bit as valuable to the side as teacher and inspiration to strike partner Fowler. Rush had lacked the natural confidence of Fowler at the same age, but once instilled with vital self-belief he wasted little time in smashing almost every scoring record Liverpool and Wales had to offer. In his first spell at Anfield he only once failed to top 30 goals in six full seasons, and won the Golden

Boot of Europe's most prolific marksman in the treble-winning year of 1984. Before moving to Juventus in 1987 he collected ten major winners' medals in just over six years.

When he returned from Italy a season later, Rush was not considered to be the same deadly goalscorer as in previous years, but he was now a far more complete player outside the box as well as in it. Tall and wiry, Rush's main attacking strengths had always been mobility, acceleration and a cool and unerring eye for goal. But he had also been famed as Liverpool's first line of defence, forever harrying defenders across the back line, refusing to allow them to settle on the ball, before forcing mistakes and regaining possession with his sharp tackling. He retained all those attributes in his second Anfield spell – in which he won a further four trophies and passed Roger Hunt's overall scoring record – but his stint in Serie A had made him a more creative player and more effective with his back to goal. Robbie Fowler learned well, but could not have asked for a better tutor.

Ian RUSH

Born:
20 October 1961
Birthplace:
St Asaph, North Wales
Height:
6ft
Weight:
12st 6lb
Position:
Striker
Games:
649
Goals:
338
Previous clubs:
Chester City, Juventus
Transfer fee:
£300,000 (to Chester),
£3.2 million
(to Juventus)
International status:
Wales international

Ian Rush heads for goal in his final season

John **Scales**

JOHN Scales was the final piece in Roy Evans's defensive jigsaw as he set about building a rearguard based around three solid centre-backs in the autumn of 1994. Scales, who actually played against Liverpool as a substitute striker for Wimbledon in the 1988 FA Cup

John Scales wins possession in a 3–2 Premiership defeat at Blackburn Rovers in 1994. Moving to Liverpool turned out to be a wise career move and he soon won an England call-up

final, arrived at Anfield with a reputation as a dominating defender who was good in the air, confident on the ground and who posed an aerial threat to the opposition when going forward for set-pieces.

In his first season Scales fully justified his build-up and his £3 million price tag, as Liverpool tightened up a previously leaky rearguard to secure the second best defensive record in the Premiership and land a record fifth League Cup. He allied coolness under pressure with good positional sense and finely-timed tackling to come through as many observers' choice as the Reds' best defender.

Injury cost him the start of the 1995–96 campaign, and the re-emergence of Mark Wright meant he did not get back into the side until around Christmas, when he played alongside Wright rather than instead of him. But once back in the line-up, he became a mainstay of the side that reached the FA Cup Final and was one of the few successes of Liverpool's defeat against Manchester United.

However, Scales turned 30 that summer and another slow-healing injury suffered pre-season ruled him out of the opening months of 1996–97. He enjoyed a brief return to first-team action after Wright frac-

John SCALES

Born:
4 July 1966
Birthplace:
Harrogate, Yorkshire
Height:
6ft 2in
Weight:
13st 5lb
Position:
Defender
Games:
94
Goals:
5
Previous clubs:
Wimbledon, Bristol City, Leeds United
Transfer fee:
£3 million
International status:
England international

tured a cheekbone in Europe, but made way for the same man as soon as he was fit to return. There was still surprise, though, when Liverpool accepted a bid of £2.6 million for the player in December 1996, until the mystery of the decision to let him go was solved by the arrival of a younger direct replacement in Bjorn Tore Kvarme.

Michael **Thomas**

AS an Arsenal player, Michael Thomas scored the last-minute goal which cost Liverpool the Championship in 1989. Yet, although he repaid some of that debt with the strike which put the Reds on their way to victory in the 1992 FA Cup final, he struggled to make the same sort of impact on the Anfield side's League ambitions as he had done for the Gunners

Thomas moved north in December 1991 to take over the attacking midfield role vacated by Steve McMahon, and completed the season with a respectable five goals from 21 games as Liverpool went on to triumph at Wembley. After that, however, injuries and selection decisions limited his first-team chances. First, a succession of minor knocks was followed by a ruptured Achilles tendon, suffered in an FA Cup tie against Bolton in 1993, which sidelined him for a year. And on his return to fitness he found John Barnes and Jamie Redknapp ahead of him in the queue for places in central midfield.

But when Redknapp's torn hamstring allowed Thomas back into the side in November 1995, it was no coincidence that Liverpool then embarked on a four-month unbeaten run taking them right into the heart of the Championship battle and the semi-finals of the FA Cup. The ex-Gunner had made his name as an attacking player who could score goals bursting into the box, but now found himself cast in a deeper-lying, holding role. That was no prob-

lem to a solid player who had started out as a defender, but when he was harshly dropped for the 1996 FA Cup semi-final in favour of the returning Redknapp, his days as a Red appeared numbered.

A couple of Italian clubs offered Thomas a contract that summer but he ultimately declined their offers, signing instead for another three years at Anfield. The 29-year-old endured mixed fortunes in 1996–97, and with further midfield signings made at the season's end his desire to play as a sweeper looked likely to offer his best chance of regular first-team football with Liverpool in future.

Michael Thomas's early Reds' career was hindered by injury, but he did score in the 1992 Cup Final

Michael THOMAS

Born: 24 August 1967
Birthplace: Lambeth
Height: 5ft 9in
Weight: 12st 6lb
Position: Midfielder
Games: 148
Goals: 11
Previous club: Arsenal
Transfer fee: £1.5 million
International status: England international

Ronnie **Whelan**

Ronnie Whelan was reaching the end of his Liverpool career as the Premiership era arrived, but many Anfield observers believe that the side then suffered because of its failure to find a successor to the skilful and committed Irishman.

In his later years at the club, Whelan was less in

evidence, both on the scoresheet and in attack, than he had been in the earliest of his 13 seasons with the Reds, but was no less effective for it. By the late 1980s he had become one of the Reds' more experienced players and duly exchanged the dazzling attacking game of his youth for a less heralded, but no less heroic, stint as midfield anchorman, grafting away in centre-field for the benefit of others.

Whelan had won four major trophies in his first two senior seasons, scoring winners in two League Cup finals and picking up a PFA Young Footballer of the Year award to boot, and had impressed with his shooting, control and wide range of perceptive passing. But with age, and the increasing maturity that finally made him an FA Cup-winning captain in 1989, he grew into a more responsible role that gave the likes of John Barnes and Peter Beardsley the solid platform on which to display the free-flowing attack he had once helped create himself.

However, during the early '90s he began to be plagued by injuries, and although he managed 40 games in the first two years of the Premiership – again demonstrating his versatility by filling in at left-back, centre-back and his original position of left midfield – he had to throw in the Anfield towel in the summer of 1994 when he moved to cut his managerial teeth with Southend United.

Mark **Wright**

FEW footballers have come quite as close to being shown the door at Anfield as Mark Wright did in 1994. And even fewer have resurrected their Liverpool careers quite as spectacularly as the tall defender went on to do.

Bought by Graeme Souness for £2 million, he was immediately made club captain and ended his first season by lifting the 1992 FA Cup. But then his for-

---

Ronnie WHELAN

Born:
25 September 1961
Birthplace:
Dublin
Height:
5ft 9in
Weight:
10st 13lb
Position:
Midfielder
Games:
477
Goals:
72
Previous clubs:
None
Transfer fee:
None
International status:
Republic of Ireland international

---

tunes nose-dived, along with those of the entire club, and after a chronic calf injury sidelined him for six months he was sent home from the 1994–95 pre-season tour. However, despite the expensive arrival of new centre-backs in the shape of Phil Babb and John Scales, things took a turn for the better at the end of the year. The injury was cured, and after returning to full fitness an injury to Scales threw him a lifeline in March 1995. Returning to the first team with a superb performance against Manchester United, he once again became an automatic choice and earned himself another England cap, four years after his last appearance for his country.

Playing as a sweeper, Wright had been voted into the all-star XI at the 1990 World Cup; and it was in the middle of a similar three-man back line that he enjoyed his Anfield renaissance. His dominance in the air – at both ends of the pitch – and the crispness of his recovery tackling continued to impress when he began his resurgence on the right of the back three, but he was at his best in the middle of the defence, where he could organise and direct operations without fear of his waning pace and vulnerability on the turn being too exposed. That it was the younger Scales rather than the veteran Wright who made way for Bjorn Tore Kvarme in January 1997, and the fact that the club saw fit to hand him a new contract just a month before his 34th birthday, reveals the full extent of his Anfield revival.

Mark Wright remains a class act at 33

Mark WRIGHT

Born:
1 August 1963
Birthplace:
Dorchester
Height:
6ft 2in
Weight:
13st 3lb
Position:
Defender
Games:
205
Goals:
10
Previous clubs:
Derby County, Southampton, Oxford United
Transfer fee:
£2 million
International status:
England international

Chapter 6
The Managers

Bill Shankly and the other pioneers

The Celtic influence on the fortunes of Liverpool FC began long before the managerial reign of Bill Shankly. For the Reds' first manager – although he never officially held the title – was Irishman John McKenna.

While John Houlding set about the business of actually founding the Anfield institution in 1892, McKenna looked after team affairs and helped steer Liverpool into the Football League at the end of their first season. Working in tandem with McKenna was W.E. Barclay, the club's secretary-manager, who had stuck with Houlding when he split from Everton.

Barclay was as fine a judge of a player as was McKenna and the seeds of Liverpool's early successes were sown by their shrewd scouting. But McKenna's most valuable signing was not a player at all. He was Sunderland secretary Tom Watson, who succeeded Barclay as head of team affairs in 1896 and guided the Reds to their first two League championships. He bought a host of early Liverpool legends including Alex Raisbeck and Elisha Scott. Watson also took his team to a losing appearance in the 1914 FA Cup Final, but died the following year.

David Ashworth succeeded Watson after the First World War and won the 1921–22 League title after assembling one of the finest of all Anfield sides. But in February 1923 he mystifyingly quit to take up the reins at lowly Oldham Athletic. His replacement was the first ex-player to manage the club, Scotsman Matt

McQueen, who had been an Anfield director since the Great War. He steered his predecessor's side to a second consecutive championship but was forced to retire in 1928 after losing a leg in a car accident.

Another long-term Liverpool servant was then appointed to the job. George Patterson had been made assistant to Tom Watson in 1908 and followed him as secretary seven years later. Now he added the role of manager to that title, only for illness to force him to relinquish control in 1936.

Sadly, the next Anfield incumbent was also to be forced into retirement by failing health. George Kay signed Liverpool legend Billy Liddell and also took the team to the 1946–47 Championship. Albert Stubbins, centre-forward in that great side, still believes that if war had not robbed Kay of seven years of his career then he would be remembered as one of the greatest of all managers.

Kay was suceeded by Don Welsh, who holds the dubious distinction of being the only Liverpool manager to be sacked. The team he inherited in 1951 was ageing but he could not introduce enough new blood of sufficient quality to avoid relegation in 1954. Failure to bounce back straight away cost him his job.

That was in 1956 and Liverpool again looked within the Anfield ranks for Welsh's replacement, offering the job to club coach and former captain Phil Taylor. However, after three near-misses in the promotion race he stepped down under the mounting strain of restoring the Reds to the top flight. Taylor may not have brought the club success on the field, but in making way for the appointment of Bill Shankly he helped prepare the ground for the footballing revolution that would alter the destiny of Liverpool FC.

Bill Shankly (1959–1974)

From the moment Bill Shankly arrived at Anfield on December 1, 1959, Liverpool FC would never be the same again. The Scot's wind of footballing change tore through the club with hurricane force to transform an outdated, unambitious second-division side into one of the giants of the English game.

Shankly's first act was to overhaul the Reds' prehistoric training ground and training methods. Long runs on the roads from Anfield to Melwood became a thing of the past, replaced by constant ball-work and the marathon five-a-side sessions that the manager had loved from his youth. One thing he did not change, though, was the backroom staff of Bob Paisley, Joe Fagan and Reuben Bennett, to whom he remained wisely loyal.

The playing staff was a different matter: within a year he had cleared out more than two whole teams'-worth from the squad. He promoted the likes of Ian Callaghan, Gerry Byrne and Roger Hunt from within, but without money to spend Shankly was up against it. Cash constraints prevented him buying Denis Law and Jack Charlton, and when the board was unwilling

Bill Shankly salutes the Liverpool fans after the FA Cup Final victory against Leeds at Wembley in 1965. In just six years the legendary manager took the Reds from Division Two to a European Cup semi-final appearance.

to break the Anfield transfer record for Ian St John in 1961 he hinted he might quit if the club's ambition did not match his own. The Saint was signed and was quickly followed by Ron Yeats. Within a year, Liverpool were back in the first division and on their way to the top.

Shankly relished marathon 5-a-side matches at Melwood

With the manager's passion mirrored on the terraces, his team roared to the Championship in 1964 and then – at long, long last – brought the FA Cup back to Anfield. Another title followed but towards the end of the decade the side begin to decline. Shankly simply rebuilt his team from scratch and went on to land another Championship and, ominously for the rest of Europe, the club's first Continental prize, the UEFA Cup in 1973

The next season, Liverpool again won the FA Cup and more glory looked set to follow. But on July 12, 1974, it was announced that Shankly had decided to retire. Liverpool – and the whole of football – was stunned. The news was received in the city with disbelief, but although the board spent weeks trying to change the manager's mind, Shankly had made his decision and stuck by it.

At 60, Shankly told the world, he was tired and wanted to go out at the top. But even his closest friends were never sure if he was telling the truth. By the end of the summer, the football-mad Scot had approached the Liverpool board about a possible return. Having appointed Bob Paisley as his successor, the directors were loathe to demote him in favour of reinstating Shankly. The dilemma of finding a new role for the former manager remained unresolved right up until his sudden death from a heart attack on September 28, 1981.

Liverpool mourned his passing but ensured his legend will always live on, not just in Anfield's Shankly Gates or the statue unveiled behind the Kop in 1997, but in the terrace chants of his name that remind those writing each new chapter in the Reds' success just where the story first began.

Bob Paisley (1974–1983)

Bob Paisley was the most successful manager in the history of English football. Sadly, he was also the most under-rated.

His record as Liverpool boss between 1974 and 1983 is quite staggering: in those nine years he won 13 major titles – three European Cups, six League Championships, one UEFA Cup and three League Cups – not to mention six Manager of the Year awards, five Charity Shields and a European Super Cup. But Bob's modest, unassuming manner denied him the full public acclaim to which he was entitled and which instead was lavished on men who, although well worthy of admiration, rarely measured up to the rarified standards that Paisley first set and then attained, year after year, across both England and Europe.

The genial former bricklayer joined Liverpool as a player in 1939 and stepped up to join the backroom staff in 1954. In the revolution that followed within a decade, Bill Shankly provided the inspiration and the public face of Liverpool FC; his right-hand man Paisley provided the shrewd tactical genius that underpinned the foundations of success. As club physio, he had an uncanny talent for instant, accurate diagnosis, the secret of which lay in the typical dedication that saw him quietly turn up at Broadgreen Hospital three afternoons a week to study the subject in detail. In an age when most of the game's sponge-carriers considered reading the back of a sticking-plaster box a medical education, Paisley was, as ever, far ahead of his time.

He demonstrated that advantage again and again after succeeding Shankly in July 1974. Wisely, he made no attempt to continue in Shankly's wisecracking style and, though he had a sharp sense of humour of his own, his trademarks became a match-day flat cap and the carpet-slippers in which he padded around the Anfield corridors during the week.

He did, though, share his predecessor's eye for a bargain and continued to groom world-class stars picked up for a song in the lower divisions. His first signing was Phil Neal and he went on to pluck from obscurity such famous names as Rush, Hansen, Grobbelaar and Nicol. But he was just as perceptive when buying big and although the likes of Dalglish, Souness and Lawrenson did not come cheaply, they repaid their investments many times over.

The timing of his team changes was just as masterful. Although proud of the club's "Anfield family" reputation, he never allowed any player to stay on past his sell-by date and employed a purchasing policy that allowed teams to evolve continuously rather than require regular major overhauls.

His predecessor continues to dominate outsiders' thoughts of the club, and when Paisley died in February 1996 it became too late to bestow on him the recognition accorded to other, less successful managers. But inside Anfield at least, nobody ever underestimates the contribution of Bob Paisley, the man who stands alone in the record-books.

Joe Fagan (1983–1985)

If Bob Paisley had the hardest act in football to follow when he succeeded Bill Shankly, then Joe Fagan's task was scarcely any easier when, aged 62, he replaced his former bootroom colleague as the new Reds' manager.

But the Liverpudlian, who had been on the Anfield backroom staff since 1958, carried on exactly where Paisley had left off. In his first season he made the Reds only the third club ever to win the title three years in succession. And as if that were not enough, Fagan's team went on to win the League and European Cups in the same season, an unprecedented treble that is unlikely ever to be repeated.

Fagan was another fine motivator and tactician, and demonstrated his skill in the transfer market on his very first day in charge when he bought Gary Gillespie from Coventry. Among the most honest of all footballing men, he often found difficulty in dealing with some of the club's more individualistic players, but he was happy to give youth its head by introducing Steve Nicol to the side in that treble-winning term.

The following season, however, the Reds struggled

Bob Paisley...the most successful manager in English football history

Many thought Joe Fagan had an impossible task in following Bob Paisley into the Liverpool hot seat. Fagan went on to win an unprecedented treble in his short career

to overcome the loss to Sampdoria of the talismanic Graeme Souness and found themselves in the relegation zone at the end of October. Fagan roused his troops to roar up the table, finishing runners-up and reaching a second consecutive European Cup Final. He had announced his decision to retire before that fateful 1985 encounter, but the horror of that evening in Heysel eclipsed what should have been the perfect send-off and saw him bow out in distraught disillusionment with the game he had loved for so long. It was the saddest possible way for him to go.

Kenny Dalglish (1985–1991)

Appointing the first player-manager in the club's history would have been a bold move by the Liverpool board at any time, let alone in the aftermath of Heysel. But in handing the job to Kenny Dalglish in the summer of 1985 they could not have chosen a better man for the task, and within a year their faith had been rewarded with the League and Cup double.

Dalglish had the wisdom of advisor Bob Paisley to call on, but immediately proved himself a fine manager in his own right, plunging into the transfer market to buy Steve McMahon as the perfect replacement for Graeme Souness and stepping into playing action himself at precisely the right moment to inspire his team on the title run-in.

While that instant triumph of 1986 had Dalglish's playing influence stamped all over it – he even scored the Championship-winning goal – Anfield's next League crown owed everything to the great Scot's growing managerial expertise. The loss of Ian Rush to

Juventus in 1987 was expected to hit Liverpool hard. Dalglish, however, made sure he was barely missed, rebuilding the team around new boys John Barnes, Peter Beardsley and John Aldridge to create arguably the most exciting and dynamic title-winning side in the club's history.

However, Dalglish's managerial career had begun in the shadow of human tragedy and in April 1989 it was hit by disaster again, as he found himself leading the club through the aftermath of Hillsborough. He, and his wife Marina, won new respect for the strength and dignity with which they and the rest of the Anfield staff helped guide the city through its grief.

Liverpool went on to lift the FA Cup that year and 12 months later claimed the third Championship and fifth trophy in all of Dalglish's five-year reign. But the Hillsborough tragedy had taken more out of him than anyone realised, and combined with the pressure of keeping the Reds at the top, the strain began to tell. A couple of unlikely signings were followed by inconsistent team selections which suggested the manager was beginning to doubt his own, normally outstanding, judgement.

Things continued to go wrong, and after a nerve-shredding 4–4 FA Cup draw at Everton in February 1991, a gaunt and drawn-looking Dalglish announced his resignation due to intolerable stress. His decision provoked equal measures of shock and sympathy throughout the city, and the reception he received on his first return to Anfield when he stepped back into management with Blackburn Rovers demonstrated the esteem in which this great football man will always be held among the Kopites.

Kenny Dalglish celebrates the 1989–90 League Championship with Ronnie Moran and Roy Evans

Graeme Souness (1991–1994)

If Bill Shankly was the whirlwind that shook Liverpool out of its complacent mediocrity in the 1960s, then the fiery Graeme Souness was the tornado, tidal wave and earthquake all rolled into one that shook Anfield to its very core three decades on. And before the dust could settle, Souness himself became the final victim of a managerial reign that was widely seen as an unnatural disaster.

When he arrived from Rangers to succeed Kenny Dalglish on April 16, 1991, he seemed an ideal choice, despite a string of high-profile disciplinary problems. As well as knowing Anfield inside out from his seven years as a player at the club, the former skipper's footballing horizons had been widened by a successful spell in Italy and he had passed his first managerial test by reaffirming Ibrox's dominance of the Scottish game. Perhaps just as importantly, a major rebuilding job was required at Liverpool and Souness seemed to possess the right blend of skill and ruthlessness to carry it out.

However, while no one expected him to make an omlette without breaking eggs, setting fire to the kitchen was not quite what had been anticipated.

Souness's passion and his love of Liverpool FC were never in doubt – Roy Evans used to fear for the manager's safety when he went home after a defeat – but his intense, almost impatient, hunger for success and hatred of mediocrity ultimately backfired to cost him his job inside three years. Although he won the FA Cup at the end of his first full season, it was continual failure (by Anfield standards) in the League, coupled with a perpetual off-field soap opera, that sealed his fate. If anything, he tried too hard.

Although continuity had been Anfield's watchword for three decades or more, the club has never been averse to change, and when Souness inherited "an old team that was going nowhere", change was indeed required. More was made than should have been of the conversion of the famous bootroom into a press lounge and alleged alterations to training routines – a charge he always denied – that resulted in an unprecedented spate of injuries.

The hot-tempered Scot had hoped to build a side based around the experience of Rush, Barnes, Whelan, Nicol, Grobbelaar and Molby, leavened with a sprinkling of the promising youngsters he found at the club. And while injuries to those key players forced him into unsettling regular team changes, personality clashes with the senior professionals also created much ill-feeling behind the scenes.

Football was stunned when Graeme Souness entered hospital for major heart surgery just days after the 1992 FA Cup semi-final. He defied doctor's orders to return to the bench for the defeat of Sunderland in the final at Wembley

Barnes was once forced into a public apology for criticising his manager in the press, while Souness himself went so far as to accuse some players of being motivated only by money. His confrontational style and the touchline antics that earned him a European ban did not endear him to some board members who feared he was endangering the club's reputation, and when the manager was given an unexpected stay of execution in May 1993, director Tony Ensor quit over the decision.

In fact, Ensor believed Souness should have resigned more than a year earlier after the incident that cost him the support of the fans. Football had been shocked by his admission to hospital for heart surgery soon after the 1992 FA Cup semi-final, but sympathy turned to scorn when he sold the story of his ordeal to The Sun, a newspaper reviled on Merseyside for its coverage of the Hillsborough disaster and which printed its exclusive on the third anniversary of the tragedy. Souness apologised, but the damage was irreparable.

Lack of on-field success further fuelled the terrace discontent and the FA Cup win of 1992 merely papered over the cracks. Souness mis-spent the bulk of the £22 million he was given for transfer fees and sold the likes of Beardsley, Houghton, Staunton and Saunders prematurely. His team failed to develop a consistent style and suffered from a loss of form on the part of several key players.

1992–93 saw a continuing slide down the League, discipline problems were translated into six sendings-off and the Reds were knocked out of the FA Cup by first-division Bolton. When Souness's programme notes for the final-day visit of Spurs were pulled at the last minute in favour of a "Thanks for your support" message from the chairman, the end seemed to be nigh, particularly as the manager was not present at the game, surfacing instead at Coventry City.

However, the following day Souness was given a remarkable and unexpected vote of confidence by the board. But within eight more turbulent months that already-fragile confidence had been shattered once again by another home FA Cup defeat, this time by Bristol City. The team were booed off the pitch, shouts of "Souness out!" rang from the stands and the following day the supporters' club called for a one-match boycott to vent the fans' dissatisfaction with the boss. It did not come to that. Two days later, on January 28, Souness offered his resignation to the board. It was unanimously accepted.

As a player, Graeme Souness's power and passion helped Liverpool dominate England and Europe. As a manager, he was frustrated by players who failed to display similar qualities

Souness later admitted some of the failings of his transfer policy and agreed that with hindsight he might have tackled some problems differently. The truth of his charge – that some of the players let him down through a lack of professionalism – will remain known only to those inside the dressing-room. His final word on his time as Liverpool boss was to say that many of his difficulties "stemmed from the fact that I was guilty of trying to make the players as passionate about the game as I was". Given the standards of commitment his own playing example set, perhaps he was always asking too much. Graeme Souness's passion for football was worthy of Bill Shankly at his best. Sadly, his man-management skills were not.

Roy Evans (1994–)

The charge levelled most regularly at Graeme Souness during his ill-starred time at the Anfield helm was that he had abandoned the traditions which had served the club so well for more than 30 years. In replacing him with Roy Evans, the Reds ensured that such an accusation would not be faced by their ninth manager since the War.

Few people are better-versed in the Anfield bootroom code than Evans, who had given Liverpool more than a quarter-century of loyal service before finally

The appointment of Roy Evans as Liverpool manager in 1994 was widely seen as a return to the stability of Shankly's bootroom set-up after the upheaval and turmoil of the Souness years

becoming the boss. Having played for England Schoolboys as a youngster, he signed professional forms with the club he had previously supported from the Kop. As a player in the early Seventies, he never quite made the Liverpool grade, managing just 11 appearances at full-back, but was quickly spotted as a potential coach – and future management material.

When Bob Paisley finally persuaded him to hang up his boots at the age of 25 and take charge of the reserves, chairman John Smith prophesied that he would one day manage the club. In topping the Central League seven times in his nine seasons with the second string Evans displayed a handy trophy-winning habit, before completing his managerial education as trainer, coach and assistant boss alongside Paisley, Fagan, Dalglish and Souness.

Evans might have stepped up after the departures of Fagan and Dalglish, but was forced to wait until Souness's tempestuous reign ended in tears. If he wanted a challenge, he had got one. And if the board wanted someone who was radically different from Souness, then they were granted their wish too. Both men had in common Liverpool's traditional will to win, but differed markedly in their approaches to securing success. Where Souness thrived on conflict and displayed an often-impetuous liking for change, Evans was calm, laid-back and exhibited a preference for evolution rather than revolution.

His first task was to put the ship back on an even keel and then steer it back to the top. That he turned things around so quickly that within three years the fans were again expecting to win the Championship is testament to his own skill rather than an indicator that things were not as bad as they looked on Souness's departure. But the manner in which Evans achieved that transformation – and the fact that the Reds did not take the titles of which they soon looked capable – suggested he might still need to add another ingredient to his managerial mix to complete part two of the task he had been given.

After taking charge in January 1994, Evans didn't announce his arrival with sweeping changes, preferring instead to assume a watching brief for the remainder of the season. He later admitted he should have acted more decisively during that honeymoon period in which, he said, things were allowed to drift. That one fault, of failing to grasp the nettle straight away, later manifested itself in other areas such as his reluctance to use substitutes too early in a game and his insistence on an 'if-it-ain't-broke-don't-fix-it' poli-

Roy Evans wasted little time in restoring stability to Anfield but the Championship remains elusive

cy instead of one that that replaces worn parts before they go wrong.

Yet Evans is sufficiently shrewd to recognise that shortcoming and could rectify it with the judgement and tactical awareness he demonstrated in his first full season in charge. The Bootle-born manager's easygoing nature would later attract criticism that he gave his young stars too much off-field latitude, but long before then he had showed he was neither prepared to tolerate indiscipline nor afraid to take tough decisions.

In 1994, the attitude problems of Mark Wright and Julian Dicks saw both players sent home by Evans from a pre-season tour. Within two months, he had sold both Dicks and fellow-bad boy Don Hutchison, and quietly eased out the ageing Bruce Grobbelaar, Steve Nicol and Ronnie Whelan. He later dropped Robbie Fowler for the start of the 1995–96 season over the young striker's laissez-faire approach to training.

And when Evans did make the first big decisions of his managerial career, they paid off in immediate trophy-winning style. Early in the 1994–95 campaign, he paid a combined £7 million for John Scales and Phil Babb to form a three-man central defence with Neil Ruddock that would form the basis of the wing-back formation which earned Liverpool a record fifth League Cup by the end of the season.

Although the investment of a then-British record £8.5 million on Stan Collymore was only a partial success at best, the comparative bargain signings of Czech international Patrik Berger and Norwegian defender Bjorn Tore Kvarme have proved Evans's wisdom in the transfer market. His decision to drop captain John Barnes and switch to a conventional 4–4–2 system in the 1997 European Cup-winners' Cup semifinal provided further evidence of his tactical acumen, although the switch again came too late to save the tie.

The 1996–97 campaign ended with both Evans and Liverpool at a crossroads, the team facing accusations of perennial underachievement and the manager admitting that he could not count on being given much longer to bring the Championship back to Anfield. Evans had the honesty to admit that further steps still had to be taken to produce a title-winning team. He also possesses the footballing sense, conviction and perceptiveness to ensure the road down which the Reds continue remains the correct one.

Chapter 7

Liverpool's Foreign Legion

Proud of their home-grown talent, Liverpool have still bought some of the most gifted overseas stars to Anfield in the 1990s

At the end of the nineteenth century, when footballers who hailed from such faraway places as Scotland were considered exotic, Liverpool led the way in importing Celtic talent to such an extent that they were known as "the team of Macs".

And when they turned their attentions further afield, it was from South Africa exclusively that their first overseas players came, before and after the Second World War. That period saw the arrival of Anfield greats such as record goalscorer Gordon Hodgson, winger Berry Nieuwenhuys and goalkeeper Arthur Riley.

Bill Shankly's distrust of fancy foreigners in the 1960s and the lure of the lira and Deutschmark in the 1970s and '80s meant the Reds bought only the occasional Continental in those days. And when they did begin taking the plunge, they bought two more South African-born players, although they did come to Anfield via Middlesbrough and Crewe. Those shrewd but conservative signings were midfielder Craig Johnston and goalkeeper Bruce Grobbelaar, and although the team that completed the League and FA Cup Double at Wembley in 1986 contained no Englishmen, that pair were the only members of the side to hail from outside the British Isles.

Since the formation of the Premiership, rising prices at home and the implementation of the Bosman ruling, which allows out-of-contract players to move between countries without a fee, have made Continental players increasingly popular. Liverpool's foreign legion is larger now than it has ever been and in the coming years is quite likely to expand further.

Patrik **Berger**

Prior to the purchase of Patrik Berger, all Liverpool's overseas signings had arrived as virtual unknowns. The £3 million Czech international was the Reds' first *bona fide* continental superstar, mainstay of the national team that had been the surprise package of Euro '96 and with a Bundesliga championship medal to prove

Czech star Patrik Berger made a superb start to his Anfield career with two goals at Leicester

Patrik BERGER

Date of birth:
10 November 1973
Place of birth:
Prague, Czech Republic
Height:
6ft 1in
Weight:
12st 6lb
Position:
Midfielder
Games:
34 (11 as sub)
Goals:
9
Previous clubs:
Sparta Prague, Slavia Prague, Borussia Dortmund
Transfer fee:
£3m in August 1996
International status:
Czech Republic international

his worth at the highest club level.

The then-22-year-old's reputation as the finest young player his country had produced – together with his glamorous looks – sparked "Bergermania" among the fans, particularly when he revealed himself as a boyhood Liverpool fan and produced the scarf and programme to prove it. His reserve team debut drew a crowd of more than 10,000, and when he scored with a trademark howitzer from 20 yards the clamour for a first-team place grew louder by the day.

A minor injury sustained just before his move from Borussia Dortmund delayed his introduction, but when it came he lived up to all the sky-high expectations that had gone before. After a brief substitute's stint against Southampton in September 1996 he was brought on for the second half of what had hitherto been a dull, goalless draw at Leicester. Berger soon changed that, adding an extra spark to Liverpool's play and blasting in two stupendous goals from the edge of the box, one of which was timed hitting the net at more than 70mph. That earned the attacking midfielder a starting place against Chelsea the following week, and a further Man of the Match display saw him hit another beautifully-taken brace in a 5–1 win.

Both player and team were still learning about one

another but his early showing was exciting enough to fill Anfield for the formality of a European tie against Finnish minnows My-Pa 47. Berger rewarded the faithful by scoring again and looked to have found his niche partnering Steve McManaman, just behind lone striker Robbie Fowler.

But as the season went on and Roy Evans shuffled his pack in search of a title-winning hand, the new hero of the Kop found himself in and out of the side and on and off the bench. Athletic, quick and skilful, he operated both up-front and wide on the left in the closing stages of his debut season, but although he impressed in scoring and creating as a second striker in the campaign's final home game, Berger still seemed best suited to the attacking midfield role in which he first appeared. As a transitional period of settling in, the year had gone as well as might have been reasonably expected. And the promise of what lay ahead meant "Bergermania" was more than a passing craze.

Stig Inge **Bjornebye**

The success at Anfield of Stig Inge Bjornebye has been a triumph of persistence and professionalism over a series of setbacks that would have had many of the Premier League's more fickle imports looking to jump ship at the earliest opportunity.

When the dedicated defender arrived on Merseyside in the winter of 1992 he must have wondered exactly what he had let himself in for. Mounting internal strife racked the Reds on an unprecedented scale and Bjornebye found himself thrown into an unsettled and uncertain side. He took the Man of the Match award on his debut but the team still lost 5–1; and after they went nine games without a win, manager Graeme Souness declined to give the new boy

Stig Inge Bjornebye took time to settle but is now one of the most consistent performers in the Liverpool side

Stig Inge BJORNEBYE	
Date of birth:	11 December 1969
Place of birth:	Elverum, Norway
Height:	5ft 10in
Weight:	11st 9lb
Position:	Defender
Games:	121 (3 as sub)
Goals:	4
Previous club:	Rosenborg
Transfer fee:	£600,000 in December 1992
International status:	Norway international

any longer to find his feet.

Bjornebye resided in the reserves until Roy Evans, taking over from Souness, spied a new role for him. Liverpool began 1994–95 fielding three centre-halves flanked by wing-backs charged with contributing in both defence and attack. The patient left-back admitted that, having been brought up on a strict diet of flat back-fours, the new arrangement was completely alien to him.

Nevertheless, he threw himself wholeheartedly into the role and compensated for what he lacked in pace through his superb left foot and the dogged determination of his defending. His crossing was a little erratic but he did well enough to miss only three of the 48 games Liverpool played en route to victory in the 1995 League Cup final.

But immediately after that triumph, misfortune struck. The Reds followed Wembley victory with a free-flowing 3–1 win over Southampton, but as Bjornebye lunged for a cross to the far post he snagged his studs in the turf and broke his leg. That cost him more than six months out, and when he returned to fitness found himself well down the queue for the left wing-back role. Although he did consider asking for a move, Stig's admirable professionalism prompted him to battle on at Anfield, where he maintained sufficiently high standards to retain his international place while trapped in Liverpool's reserves.

Then, at the start of 1996–97, injuries to others gave

him another chance. He took it with both hands, scoring the first goal of the Premiership season and going on to be an ever-present and arguably Liverpool's best and most consistent performer. Now looking totally at ease with the wing-back role, the waywardness vanished from his crossing to make him one of the League's leading providers of scoring chances. And having finally found his feet, there should still be much, much more to come.

Bruce **Grobbelaar**

See Premiership Stars page 58

Glenn **Hysen**

Few players could match the peerless Alan Hansen for calm and grace under pressure, but for a season at least Glenn Hysen went gratifyingly close as the pair helped Liverpool to the 1989–90 League Championship. Hysen, rated in the late 1980s as the finest defender

The classy Glenn Hysen helped Liverpool to the title in 1989–90 before age caught up with him

Glenn HYSEN

Date of birth:
30 October 1959
Place of birth:
Gothenburg, Sweden
Height:
6ft 1in
Weight:
12st 8lb
Position:
Defender
Games:
83 (2 as sub)
Goals:
3
Previous clubs:
Warta, IFK Gothenburg,
PSV Eindhoven,
Fiorentina
Transfer fee:
£600,000 in July 1989
International status:
Sweden international

Sweden had ever produced, was popular with the Anfield fans before he even played a game, for he had been snatched from Fiorentina under the noses of arch-rivals Manchester United.

Hysen's pedigree, which included two UEFA Cup wins as well as a couple of successful seasons in Serie A, raised expectations among the fans; but a high-class debut in the Charity Shield suggested the £600,000 raid on Florence had been worthwhile. And so, at first it proved, as his experience and quality gelled nicely with Hansen's class. The silver-haired Hysen was powerful in the air, comfortable on the ball and as cool in possession as his partner at the heart of the defence.

The title returned to Anfield that year, and although Hansen was forced to retire through injury there seemed little reason why the tall Swede could not assume his mantle. Hysen was even handed the club captaincy for a spell, but all of a sudden his advancing years appeared to catch up with him. Where initially he had looked commanding and certain, he now appeared vulnerable and troubled by the pace of the English game. Certainly, when Graeme Souness succeeded Kenny Dalglish in the early part of 1991 he made it immediately clear that Hysen should start checking his pension arrangements.

The firebrand Scot favoured a new defensive line-up built around the skill of Jan Molby, dropped Hysen for his first game in charge and then bought Mark Wright in the summer break. Disillusioned the following term by a situation in which he was given just two starts before Christmas – although he scored on one of them, in a home defeat by Crystal Palace – he spoke out about the growing divisions inside the Anfield dressing room.

Within a month he was handed a free transfer and at the end of the season he took the offer up, returning to his home town of Gothenburg with Swedish first division side GAIS. The 1990 Championship trophy

nestling on the Anfield sideboard was a fair measure of Hysen's success as a short-term investment, but the 30th birthday he celebrated within a couple of months of his arrival emphasised that he was always living on borrowed time.

Istvan **Kozma**

Quite why Graeme Souness bought Istvan Kozma from Dunfermline in 1992 remains one of the larger mysteries of his time at the Anfield helm, although what a Hungarian international who had been plying his trade in France was doing in the nether regions of the Scottish Premier League in the first place is equally imponderable.

Kozma, a midfielder who could also operate up-front, had been admired for some time by Souness, who liked him so much he had twice tried unsuccessfully to sign him while at Rangers. What had impressed him most was the ease with which he had coped with the helter-skelter of Scottish football, which made even the game south of the border look Continentally-paced in comparison. Although Kozma had scored only twice in 32 games for Dunfermline, he had a reputation as a free-kick expert and was expected to bring the virtues of pace, skill, vision, athleticism and excellent ball control with him to Liverpool.

He may well have possessed all those talents and

Istvan Kozma was a surprise signing by Souness in 1992

Istvan KOZMA

Date of birth:
3 December 1964
Place of birth:
Paszto, Hungary
Height:
5ft 9in
Weight:
12st
Position:
Midfielder
Games:
10 (4 as sub)
Goals:
0
Previous clubs:
Ujpest Doza, Bordeaux,
Dunfermline
Transfer fee:
£300,000
International status:
Hungary international

more, but the fans at Anfield never really got to see them, as he played just nine times in his 18 months at the club. He inspired a Liverpool fightback from the embarrassment of a 3–0 deficit at home to lowly Chesterfield as a second-half League Cup substitute in September 1992, but that was about the only significant contribution he was allowed to make.

At the end of the season it came as little surprise when the Department of Employment declined to renew his work permit – which was dependent on the applicant having played in 75 per cent of the matches for which he was available – and the Reds had to write off his £300,000 transfer fee as he returned to Hungary with Ujpesti Te on a free.

Souness claimed Kozma was a victim of circumstances, in that he had been bought as a player who would make a good team better, but was of little value to the strugglers of that Anfield vintage. On the limited evidence available, the bemused fans had to take his word for it.

Bjorn Tore **Kvarme**

Christmas came late to Liverpool in the 1996–97 season, but when a gift did arrive from the fringes of Lapland it proved well worth the wait. Bjorn Tore Kvarme impressed in a brief trial at the beginning of December, and by holding off for a month until his contract with Norwegian champions Rosenborg expired in the New Year, Liverpool were able to save £2 million by signing him on a free transfer under the Bosman ruling.

Kvarme should not have been a complete unknown to Liverpool, as he had scored against them in a pre-season friendly five years earlier. Then he had been playing on the right wing for Rosenborg, but his career only really took off when he switched to right-back the following season.

Bjorn Tore Kvarme proved the find of the 1996–97 season after arriving at Anfield on a free transfer

Bjorn Tore KVARME	
Date of birth:	17 June 1972
Place of birth:	Trondheim, Norway
Height:	6ft 1in
Weight:	12st 6lb
Position:	Defender
Games:	16
Goals:	0
Previous club:	Rosenborg
Transfer fee:	None, signed in January 1997
International status:	Norway under-21 international

That was the role in which the Reds first spotted him, and their interest was quickly confirmed by the versatility he showed in switching to centre-back as his team pulled off a shock 1–0 European Cup win over AC Milan at San Siro.

Liverpool signed the tall, rangy defender as a long-term replacement for Mark Wright, but the instant impression his tough tackling made in training earned him a debut just hours after his international clearance came through. Kvarme's quality in the timing of his challenges, his excellent anticipation, perceptive reading of the play and intelligent use of the ball were immediately obvious, as was his electric pace in a game against Aston Villa that Liverpool won 3–0.

A rude awakening swiftly followed in a 4–2 FA Cup defeat at Chelsea but, as he adjusted to the pace of the English game and his defensive colleagues tuned in to his preference for using the ball constructively under pressure rather than simply hoofing it

Defender Torben Piechnik came to Liverpool after helping Denmark to a surprise European Championship triumph against Germany in 1992

into the stand, he became more and more influential and took three Man of the Match awards – including one from his Merseyside derby debut – from the 16 matches he played. And when the Reds switched to a flat back-four in the season's closing stages, Kvarme not only retained a place at right-back but performed well enough to be preferred to England international Rob Jones in the role.

That was an impressive start to his Liverpool career, but was not good enough for the player himself. The one flaw in his game had been a vulnerability under the high ball, in both positioning and heading. Typically, instead of heading for the beach at the season's end, Kvarme took himself off to Norway to spend the summer working on that aspect of his game. Liverpool should reap the dividends of his dedication for many years to come.

Jan **Molby**

See Premiership Stars page 63

Torben **Piechnik**

Torben PIECHNIK	
Date of birth:	21 May 1963
Place of birth:	Copenhagen, Denmark
Height:	6ft
Weight:	12st 4lb
Position:	Defender
Games:	24
Goals:	0
Previous club:	FC Copenhagen
Transfer fee:	£600,000 in September 1992
International status:	Denmark international

With transfer fees in the domestic market of the early 1990s already over-inflated and continuing to rise, Liverpool began looking further afield for more sensibly priced talent. And on the lookout for a top-quality centre-back, manager Graeme Souness's eye was caught by the imposing figure of Danish international Torben Piechnik.

The FC Copenhagen star had impressed during his country's fairy-tale run to an unexpected triumph in the 1992 European Championships, and when Souness took a further look at him in another game against the German side they had beaten 2–0 in the final, his initial impression appeared to be con-

firmed. A £600,000 deal was done and Liverpool looked to have got themselves an experienced international talent at a bargain price.

Piechnik was quick, strong and good in the air, and at first looked able to fill in as either a sweeper or a stopper. An injury to Mark Wright meant he got his chance alongside Steve Nicol, and after the Reds had leaked seven goals in his first two games they began to strike up a promising partnership. But by Christmas, a slump in the team's form was matched by a similar falling off in Piechnik's game. When he was sidelined by a hamstring injury in January, the Reds were relieved that Wright was ready to resume normal service. Wright and Nicol continued to the end of the season, and when Souness plunged into the summer transfer market to snap up Neil Ruddock from Tottenham, he sent Piechnik a clear message that his Anfield days were numbered.

The tall Dane was given a run against Newcastle United early the following season, but with his 30th birthday behind him and the Reds losing 3–0 on his return he knew he was occupying the bed nearest the door. In the summer he accepted the inevitable and returned to his homeland by joining Aarhus on a free transfer. If Piechnik had been more expensive in 1992, Liverpool might have thought twice about buying him in the first place, rather than choosing to take what looked like only a modest gamble at the time. Hindsight reveals that for once the club's legendary eye for real quality at a bargain price had momentarily deserted it.

Ronnie **Rosenthal**

In the 1970s, David Fairclough's propensity for stepping off the bench to win games in their dying minutes saddled him with a "Supersub" tag he found more of a burden than a boon. In the 1990s, Ronnie Rosenthal suffered from the same affliction, although in his case the reputation was more illusory than apt.

Whereas Fairclough regularly changed single matches as a substitute, Rosenthal turned the course of an entire season with his late introduction to the Liverpool cause in March 1990. Add to that feat an injury-time winner in the derby three years later and the legend was complete. Yet in truth, the Israeli international is remembered for those priceless interventions because the remainder of his Anfield career, particularly in the Premiership years, passed largely

Ronnie ROSENTHAL

Date of birth:
11 October 1963
Place of birth:
Haifa, Israel
Height:
5ft 11ins
Weight:
12st 13lb
Position:
Forward
Games:
93 (46 as sub)
Goals:
16
Previous clubs:
Maccabi Haifa, FC
Bruges, Standard Liège
Transfer fee:
£500,000 in June 1990
International status:
Israel international

without incident.

The player himself maintained he was never given the run in the starting line-up he needed to establish himself, and that claim must be given some credence in light of the fact that he never began more than five games in succession during nearly four years at the club. And even during that sequence – in which he scored at a rate of a goal a game – he was substituted three times himself.

Rosenthal arrived at Anfield on loan from Standard Liège with a couple of months of the 1989–90 season left to play and Liverpool's Championship challenge beginning to falter. He was a fast, direct forward who, like Fairclough before him, always appeared on the verge of losing control of the ball in his headlong dash for goal before somehow composing himself at the last minute to score. Yet however ungainly his style, there was no disputing its initial effectiveness. Rosenthal scored a classic hat-trick – right foot, left foot and header – on his full debut at Charlton, while the seven goals he scored in the five games he started played a major part in bringing the Reds a record 18th title and earned him a permanent move in the summer.

But after his explosive entrance, it was not hard to see why first Dalglish and then Souness preferred to keep him in reserve on the bench. For when he did play from the outset, Rosenthal appeared to lack the urgency and directness that distinguished his game as a substitute. It soon became clear that Souness saw such form as the norm rather than the exception, and in January 1994 the striker took a pay cut to move to Spurs in search of regular football. That he did not get it suggests the Liverpool manager was right.

Israeli Ronnie Rosenthal gave vital late momentum to Liverpool's title challenge as a loan signing in 1989–90, but he failed to become the influence once he joined the club permanently

Chapter 8

The Stars of the Future

With transfer markets undergoing a radical change in the 1990s, Liverpool are at the forefront of youth development in England

In the glory years of the 1960s and '70s, as far as the Reds were concerned a youth policy was something the government might come up with to combat juvenile crime. In the words of former chief scout Geoff Twentyman, the aim was "to buy young players who were three-quarters of the way there and bring them on in the reserves." That strategy unearthed such gems as Kevin Keegan, Ray Clemence and Alan Hansen, but meant the likes of Ian Callaghan, Tommy Smith and Phil Thompson, who all joined straight from school, were the exceptions rather than the rule.

Since 1984, when Liverpool's Centre of Excellence opened, all that has changed, and first-teamers Robbie Fowler, Steve McManaman and Dominic Matteo have all been associated with the club since before their teens. The FA Youth Cup win of 1996 suggested there is more hand-reared talent on its way and the £8 million invested in a new Ajax-style soccer academy, due to open in Kirkby before the Millennium, demonstrates the new emphasis on youth. The centre, designed after fact-finding missions to Amsterdam and Auxerre and to be run by Director of Youth Steve Heighway, will provide accommodation for players as well as state-of-the-art training and coaching facilities.

Steve McManaman (left) and Dominic Matteo (right) have both graduated from the youth side

Centre of Excellence

When the present Centre of Excellence began its work it had just six scouts and three coaches looking after around 50 youngsters. By the mid-1990s, there were around 120 juniors on the books, the coaching staff had expanded to 12 and 32 scouts cover the 25-mile-radius catchment area to which they are restricted by FA rules. When the project first began, its progress was hindered by a shortage of appropriate facilities and – surprisingly enough – players. In 1984, Sunday league and schools football still took precedence over professional coaching and so the Reds had only third call on the best youngsters, many of whom were playing up to 120 games a year.

Liverpool's extensive scouting network picked up Robbie Fowler when he was still a schoolboy

Today, no junior is allowed to play more than 60 matches a season and the club is able to select boys from the age of nine. The coaches are looking for those, says youth co-ordinator Frank Skelly, with the qualities of "talent, ability, balance and speed". No 11-a-side games are allowed until the youngsters reach 13, which the club calls "the age of understanding". Before then, the emphasis is placed firmly on technique and touch, but at that point they hope their players will be able to pass and control a ball, get out of certain situations and demonstrate comprehension of how to play in a team scenario. Each youngster must meet set standards to progress from one age group to another at the centre. Pupils are also given advice and literature on responding to injuries. Those who progress through the system reach the YTS or junior ranks at 16, with the ultimate aim being to attain a sufficiently high standard to sign professional forms on their 17th birthday.

Rocketing transfer fees have raised the importance of the junior set-up's work, which has already saved the club upwards of £20 million in producing players of the standard of McManaman and Fowler. With the Reds' scouting network being expanded to cover the four corners of the globe in the search for recruits for the new academy, Liverpool's dream of possessing a depth of young talent to rival that of Ajax could become a reality sooner rather than later.

FA Youth Cup Winners 1996

The fruits of Liverpool's ambitious youth policy should be the eventual arrival in the first team of a bumper crop of home-grown talent. In the meantime, the capture of the FA Youth Cup for the first time in the club's history was a welcome measure of the success of the programme.

More than 20,000 fans turned out at Anfield for the second leg of the final victory over West Ham United, which turned out to be one of the less eventful encounters of the youngsters' cup run – if only by the rollercoaster standards they had set in the earlier rounds. Michael Owen's 11 goals in five games – including a match-winning hat-trick against favourites Manchester United in the quarter-final – fired the Reds to ultimate victory, but the Under-18 side impressed collectively with their teamwork, determination and refusal to buckle under pressure as much as with their considerable skill.

After wins over Bradford City, Luton Town and Sheffield United, Liverpool had looked to be heading for a last-eight exit against Manchester United before they hit back to win a thrilling encounter with a goal in the last minute. But their passage into the final itself was even more nerve-racking for players and spectators alike. A comfortable 4–2 first leg win at Anfield, featuring another hat-trick from Owen, looked to have settled the issue against Crystal Palace. However, with 48 minutes of the second leg gone, Liverpool found themselves 3–0 down and staring aggregate defeat in the face, before Jamie Cassidy grabbed a vital goal to force extra time, in which another brace from Owen completed the job.

Liverpool won the first leg of the final 2–0 at Upton Park and although they conceded a goal after just 51 seconds of the Anfield return, goals from Owen and winger Stuart Quinn sealed a famous victory.

The squad that clinched the trophy was: Roy Naylor, Lee Prior, Phil Brazier (captain), Jamie Carragher, Gareth Roberts, Stuart Quinn, David Thompson, Mark Quinn, Jamie Cassidy, John Newby, Michael Owen, Eddie Turkington, Andy Parkinson and Ian Dunbavin.

New faces at Anfield
Michael **Owen**

On the day Robbie Fowler scored his 100th Liverpool goal to join the select band of Anfield centurions, a new chapter in the story of the club's great strikers was quietly opened. For the first time, the name of Michael Owen appeared on the senior squad sheet.

Michael OWEN

Date of birth: 14 December 1979
Place of birth: Hawarden
Position: Striker
Games: 2 (1 as sub)
Goals: 1
International honours: England Youth, U-20, U-18

Michael Owen was playing for Liverpool at 17

The date was that of his 17th birthday and the fact that the Reds were so keen to promote him to the first-team ranks the instant he signed a professional contract reveals how highly he is rated at Anfield. And when he eventually made his debut, as a substitute at Wimbledon in May 1997, he showed the world exactly why. Within 16 minutes of taking the field he ran onto Bjornebye's through ball to become Liverpool's youngest-ever scorer with a single, confident touch before later forcing a full-length save from Dons keeper Neil Sullivan and almost carving out a last-gasp equaliser with an inviting cross that two of his colleagues somehow failed to convert.

But the slightly-built former FA School of Excellence pupil has the pedigree to support his star billing. Playing for Deeside Schools against boys often three years older than him, he smashed Ian Rush's record of 72 goals in a season by a clear 20 and passed the previous best for appearances – held by Everton's Gary Speed – as he clocked up a total of 148 goals in 115 games. He has broken England's scoring records at Under-15 and Under-16 level, scored a winner against Brazil, hit 11 goals in five games to fire Liverpool to their first-ever FA Youth Cup triumph, taken his country into the finals of the mini-World Cup and, after joining the Reds full-time in 1996, found the net 30 times in his first 25 games.

Owen's record said he was ready for the first team at the age of 17 and, just as importantly, his ability and character said he could handle it too. His coaches cite his speed of both movement and thought, and his bravery, aggression and instinctive eye for goal as the key technical components of his game, but say it is his attitude and composure that mark him out as something special at such an early age. Although they stress that they are still only talking about potential just yet, there seems no escaping the fact that the goal he scored at Wimbledon looks certain to be the first of very, very many.

Jamie **Carragher**

Few Liverpool debutants can have made as immediate an impact as did Jamie Carragher on his introduction to the Premiership – and even fewer can have done so at the tender age of 18.

The England Under-21 international had been given a game against Everton in a pre-season friendly and added an hour of senior substitute action to that experience midway through the 1996–97 season before an injury to John Barnes handed him a first League start for the visit of Aston Villa. Not only did Carragher look instantly at home in the first team but he also wasted little time in adding a bit of bite to the Reds' midfield, dumping the experienced Andy Townsend on to the seat of his shorts with a fierce tackle that earned him a booking inside 30 seconds.

If that showed that the Bootle boy had the physical presence to succeed in the top flight, then the way he reacted to that yellow card and used the ball throughout the remainder of the game demonstrated that he has the intelligence for it too. Carragher impressed with his work rate and passing, but capped his afternoon by heading the goal that put Liverpool on their way to a handsome 3–0 win.

The 1996 winner of Liverpool's Young Player of the

Year award first came to attention in the Reds' Youth Cup-winning team after graduating from the FA's National School. Ironically, Carragher stood out as the biggest of that Anfield bunch, for at Lilleshall he was the least physically imposing of his peers. But it was the youngster's skill, vision and footballing brain rather than his size that got him into the school and he has lost none of that while filling out. Although not the quickest of players, he has a priceless ability to get himself in the right place at the right time, while the quality of his passing is stamped through with the Anfield hallmark.

Central midfield is his favoured position, although he also shone while filling in at centre-back during the later stages of the 1996 Youth Cup campaign. His anticipation, tackling and distribution from the back won him widespread plaudits and could well have prompted the thought among the Anfield coaches that he may not yet have found his best position. With the summer of 1997 spent playing for England Under-18s in the mini-World Cup, he should be even better equipped to stake his claim to more senior action.

> **Jamie CARRAGHER**
>
> **Date of birth:** 28 January 1978
> **Place of birth:** Bootle
> **Position:** Midfielder
> **Games:** 3 (2 as sub)
> **Goals:** 1
> **International honours:** England Youth, U-18, U-21

Local boy Jamie Carragher celebrates scoring on his full debut against Aston Villa in January 1997

David **Thompson**

> **David THOMPSON**
>
> **Date of birth:** 12 September 1977
> **Place of birth:** Birkenhead
> **Position:** Midfield
> **Games:** 2 (both as substitute)
> **Goals:** 0
> **International honours:** England Youth, U-18, U-21

Midfielder David Thompson has been promoted to the Liverpool first team squad on the grounds that if you are good enough you are not just old enough, but big enough too.

Standing just 5ft 7ins tall and weighing in at a lightweight 10 stones, the Birkenhead-born youngster cut a diminutive figure in junior football, let alone on the Premiership stage on to which he stepped as a substitute in 1996–97. But his skill and determination left the Anfield staff in no doubt that he could cope with the step up.

Thompson was given a run of just three minutes at the end of Liverpool's 2–0 home win over Arsenal in August 1996, but when he was sent on in the following Saturday's goalless draw against Sunderland he almost made an immediate name for himself. Though only on the pitch for five minutes, the youngster got sufficiently involved to have a shot at goal and get his name taken for dissent. That sort of determination has made him a driving force in each of the Anfield nursery teams in which he has played since joining the club's School of Excellence after his natural ability with both feet at the age of just nine caught the eye of youth coach Hugh McAuley.

Thompson, who made his England Under-21 debut against Poland in October 1996, became a reserve team regular at the age of 17 and instantly showed the confidence to chivvy along some of his more senior colleagues in the side. That sort of self-belief has aided his rise through the ranks, but the former Merseyside Schools star has the skill to justify it. As well as physical courage, Thompson is noted for his excellent vision, good control and his accurate, perceptive passing over all distances. He also possesses a fierce and accurate shot, which he showed to good effect in scoring a stunning 20-yarder to help keep Liverpool Reserves in the top flight with a vital win over Everton on the last day of the 1996–97 campaign.

He was the first of the Reds' FA Youth Cup-winners to graduate to the first team squad when a spate of injuries and international calls saw him included as a 18-year-old in the party that travelled to Bolton in December 1995. Thompson was not involved that day but will no doubt get another chance in the near future.

Chapter 9

The Great League Matches

While the drama of cup football has meant many of Liverpool's most memorable moments have come in knock-out competitions, their astonishing success in the League has also produced its fair share of matches to live long in the memory.

The Reds' early years produced some high-scoring classics and their regular meetings with neighbours Everton could always be guaranteed to produce fireworks. But it was after the Second World War – and particularly from the 1960s on – that Liverpool's relentless accumulation of titles produced the majority of the finest performances in the club's proud history.

When football resumed in September 1946, the first post-war Championship came to Anfield the following spring and the win that put Liverpool top of the final table was a real thriller. They travelled to second-placed Wolverhampton Wanderers with both sides requiring a win to clinch the title, providing fellow contenders Stoke City lost at Sheffield United a fortnight later.

Stoke did indeed slip up and Liverpool took the crown thanks to their win at Molineux clinched by a pre-planned and perfectly executed goal. The Reds took an early lead through Jack Balmer and just before

Liverpool captain Emlyn Hughes celebrates the 1975–76 League Championship title with his team-mates after the 3–1 defeat of Wolverhampton Wanderers at Molineux started a run of four championships in five seasons

half-time winger Bob Priday, in response to an earlier tactical discussion, dropped deep and clipped a long ball over the head of Stan Cullis. Striker Albert Stubbins raced onto the ball in the centre circle and charged half the length of the pitch before beating two defenders and the goalkeeper to score. Wolves pulled one back after the break to set up a grandstand finish but Liverpool held out to win the game and the League.

Nearly 30 years later, Liverpool were involved in what was almost a repeat Championship finish on the same ground. This time, in 1976, they needed a win from their final game to overhaul Queens Park Rangers and snatch the title by a point. It seemed half of Merseyside had packed itself behind the Molineux goal to cheer Bob Paisley's men on, but by half-time they looked likely to be disappointed as their heroes trailed 1–0 and the pressure appeared to be telling on them. But late goals from Kevin Keegan, John Toshack and Ray Kennedy triggered title celebrations that went on into the night, turning a football traffic-jammed M6 into a raucous street party with the team bus as its focal point.

Liverpool's blend of power and skill had earlier brought them twin Championship success in the 1960s, and the game that clinched the 1963–64 competition proved an Anfield classic as Arsenal were swept aside in a 5–0 drubbing inspired by two-goal winger Peter Thompson. But the Gunners gained their revenge 25 years later when Anfield hosted the most dramatic title finish in history. Arsenal needed to win 2–0 to deny Liverpool a double double and did so with the last kick of the season as their physically and emotionally drained opponents succumbed to the programme of eight games in 23 days they had gone through after returning to action following the Hillsborough disaster.

Capital Clashes

Liverpool's clashes with their rivals from the capital have always produced memorable matches, but none more so than the Reds' famous 7–0 thrashing of Tottenham Hotspur in September 1978. The Londoners' capture of Argentinian World Cup stars Osvaldo Ardiles and Ricardo Villa had been the talk of the pre-season, but they were given a withering welcome from a Liverpool team with which any side in the world would have struggled to live that afternoon.

Two goals from Kenny Dalglish started the rout, which continued with two more from substitute David Johnson and one apiece from Ray Kennedy and Phil Neal before Terry McDermott rounded off the scoring with one of the greatest goals ever seen at Anfield. Goalkeeper Ray Clemence turned defence into attack with a clearance to Johnson, who moved possession quickly on to Heighway on the left. While the move was progressing, McDermott was tearing forward down the right, sprinting from one set of posts to the other to meet Heighway's perfect cross with an unstoppable header. Few Anfield regulars expect to see that goal bettered.

Another capital classic came on the final day of the 1985–86 campaign, when Liverpool clinched the first leg of their famous League and FA Cup double with a tense 1–0 win at Chelsea courtesy of a magnificent goal from player-manager Kenny Dalglish. The Scottish maestro had effectively hung up his boots by the time the Reds took the Championship again two years later, but the team he created went down in Anfield history as perhaps the most exciting the club had seen. The 1987–88 champions, built around new boys John Barnes and Peter Beardsley, equalled the Leeds record of 29 League games unbeaten from the start of the season and provided the sell-out crowds that flocked to see them with goals and magic galore.

The Reds were rarely anything less than rampant in losing only twice all season, but the highest points came early and late in the campaign. A free-flowing 4–1 televised September win at Newcastle United, in which Steve Nicol scored a spectacular hat-trick, preceded three successive 4–0 wins, the last of which was the most awe-inspiring. Title hopefuls QPR arrived at Anfield expected to give the Reds a serious test only to be blown away by a virtuoso performance from Barnes, who struck two majestic goals, one of which capped a swaying, jinking run from the halfway line.

Impressing the Preston Plumber

The greatest performance of that memorable season was a 5–0 destruction of high-flying Nottingham Forest at Anfield in April 1988. Tom Finney, the former England and Preston star, described it as the finest performance he had ever seen and few present that night felt disposed to argue after two goals from John Aldridge and further finishes from Ray Houghton, Peter Beardsley and Gary Gillespie completed the footballing masterclass.

Two seasons later, Liverpool, although not reaching quite the same heights of total football, surpassed that Nottingham Forest score when they beat hapless Crystal Palace 9–0 on a night that saw Aldridge say his farewells to Anfield, signing off with a penalty to add to goals from Nicol (two) McMahon, Rush, Gillespie, Beardsley, Barnes and Hysen.

A 4–0 home win over Manchester United featuring an audacious Beardsley hat-trick was the outstanding memory of the campaign, and as the Premiership era was ushered in Liverpool deprived United of the last Football League Championship win with a final day Anfield victory in 1991–92 that handed the title to Leeds United.

The Great Games of the Premiership Years

4 January 1994
FA Premiership
LIVERPOOL 3
MANCHESTER UNITED 3

While the match that bade farewell to the standing Kop was something of an anti-climax as the Reds went down 1–0 to Norwich City, the final night League game to be played in front of the famous old terrace stood comparison with any of the great evenings it had ever seen.

The action that unfolded over a breathless 90 minutes quite befitted the deafeningly partisan atmosphere in which it took place and ended with Reds fans roaring with pride at one of the greatest comebacks in the club's history. Even before kick-off, a special night was in prospect as the Kop showed the world that it was still the best – even if its team had fallen on relatively hard times. The terrace glowed red with the glare of a clutch of maritime rescue flares that belched a continental-style fog of red smoke out from under the roof to envelope the pitch. Flags waved, You'll Never Walk Alone rang out at spine-tingling volume and a giant banner moved across the crowd to remind the visiting league champions that "Form is Temporary, Class is Permanent".

No player could fail to be inspired by the scene but the roar that greeted a chance for teenager Robbie Fowler after just 47 seconds seemed to startle him into fluffing his opportunity. Liverpool

LIVERPOOL 3 MAN UNITED 3 (ht 2 – 3)
Venue: Anfield
Att: 42,795
Liverpool: Grobbelaar, Jones, Wright, Ruddock, Dicks, McManaman (Bjornebye, 77), Redknapp, Clough, Barnes, Fowler, Rush (Subs not used: Nicol, James.)
Manchester United: Schmeichel, Parker, Bruce, Pallister, Irwin, Kanchelskis, Keane, Ince, McClair, Giggs, Cantona. (Subs not used: Robson, Sealey, Ferguson.)
Goals: Bruce (8), Giggs (20), Irwin (23), Clough (25, 36), Ruddock (79).
Referee: P. Don (Middlesex)

Nigel Clough scores the second of his two goals to bring Liverpool back into the match against United

continued with a passion and purpose to match that of the crowd but against a United side that specialized in lightning counter-attack they were punished for their very first mistake. Poor defensive work after eight minutes allowed Eric Cantona to cross dangerously and Steve Bruce, unmarked in front of goal, headed the visitors in front.

Momentarily taken aback, the crowd urged Liverpool on again, only for another error to put them two behind. Fowler had shot straight at Schmeichel before Jamie Redknapp's under-hit back-pass allowed Ryan Giggs to skip past Wright and lob the most delicious chip beyond Grobbelaar and into the far corner of the net.

If that was a shock for the home fans, there was worse to come within three minutes. Ruddock fouled Keane and from 20 yards out on the left of the penalty box, Denis Irwin lashed the unstoppable free-kick into the roof of the net. Anfield was stunned. The Reds had dominated the opening quarter yet found themselves 3–0 down and staring a rout in the face.

Then, with the home fans still reeling, came instant salvation. Just two minutes after the goal Nigel Clough revived his team by pouncing on a loose ball and finding the back of the Kop end net with a stunning 25-yarder. The mild-mannered Clough was fired up to the point of earning a booking for a foul on Giggs and was now first to everything, including another loose ball that he again blasted past Schmeichel to bring Liverpool within touching distance on 36 minutes.

Saves from both Grobbelaar and Schmeichel prevented the half-time score making even more astonishing reading, and both keepers pulled off further heroics in a second period that yielded fewer goals but no less excitement. Grobbelaar's amazing reflexes kept out Giggs and then Keane while Schmeichel went full length to deny Redknapp before clutching successive drives from Julian Dicks.

Liverpool were still convinced the game was not beyond them and the introduction of Stig Inge Bjornebye paid an instant dividend. Having been on the pitch for just two minutes, he sent in a perfect cross that Neil Ruddock bravely forced over the line to cap an appropriately passionate floodlit farewell to football's most passionate terrace.

Jan Molby scores the first of Liverpool's six goals

FA Premiership
20 August 1994
LIVERPOOL 6
CRYSTAL PALACE 1

The FA's fixture computer has a long-time habit of welcoming newcomers to the top flight by sending them out to face Liverpool at the earliest opportunity. A year earlier, Swindon Town were introduced to the ways of the world by a visit from the Reds that left them pondering a 5–0 spanking. This time it was the turn of First Division champions Crystal Palace, and they received six of the best in a footballing lesson that would have had almost every team in the country pleading for mercy.

LIVERPOOL 6
CRYSTAL PALACE 1 (ht 3–0)

Venue:
Anfield

Att:
18,084

Liverpool:
James, Jones, Nicol, Ruddock, Bjorneby, McManaman, Redknapp, Molby (Thomas 86), Barnes, Rush, Fowler.
Subs not used: Harkness, Stensgaard.

Crystal Palace:
Martyn, Pitcher, Young, Coleman, Gordon, Salako, Southgate, Wilkins (Bowry 80), Rodger, Armstrong, Preece (Dyer 26). Sub not used: Wilmot.

Goals: Molby (12, pen), McManaman (14, 70), Fowler (45), Armstrong (49), Rush (60, 73).

Referee: R. Hart (Darlington)

While Palace were celebrating a return to the top flight after a one-season sabbatical below stairs, Liverpool welcomed back Jan Molby, who had been missing from the Premiership scene for almost as long, having been sidelined for eight months with a calf injury. The big Dane looked at least a shade over his ideal fighting weight, but made light of that handicap with a peerless display of footballing artistry that inspired his team to their crushing victory. He provided the passing, his younger team-mates the necessary movement to rip Palace to shreds.

Molby opened the scoring himself with another of his unstoppable penalties after Simon Rodger was adjudged to have fouled Rob Jones in the box. But the second goal was a gem as the perceptive Molby timed exquisitely his short, but perfectly-weighted, pass to send McManaman racing through to curl home his first competitive goal in 363 days – since the previous year's visit to Swindon, in fact.

Fowler got in on the act, on the stroke of half-time, to capitalize on Darren Pitcher's slice and score with his left foot. Although Chris Armstrong's header reduced the arrears soon after the break, it was soon one-way traffic again. Molby was understandably beginning to tire and so fellow-Scandinavian Stig Inge Bjornebye took his turn as creator by taking Barnes' pass down the left and crossing for Rush to finish with a textbook header.

The Reds continued to play an expansive brand of football and added a fifth goal when Redknapp pulled the ball back from the bye-line for McManaman to double his tally. Not to be outdone, Rush grabbed his second with a far-post header at a corner three minutes later to get Liverpool's season off to the highest-flying of starts.

FA Premiership
4 March 1995
LIVERPOOL 2
NEWCASTLE UNITED 0

On the face of it, a run of just one defeat in 22 games going into this crunch clash looked the sort of form to give a team of Liverpool's pedigree a chance of the Championship with two months of the season left to go. But a run of three draws and a shock home defeat by an Ipswich side that had leaked nine goals at Old Trafford left visitors Newcastle United the bookmakers' stronger fancies as title contenders.

In 90 minutes of exhilarating attack, Roy Evans' Reds shattered that illusion and reasserted their own claims to the Premiership throne. Under former Anfield idol Kevin Keegan, Newcastle had earned a reputation as the League's entertainers through their total insistence on always putting the emphasis on attack. They travelled to Merseyside in typically positive mood but, when Liverpool fought fire with fire, the Magpies suddenly found themselves an endangered species.

Only one of the finest displays of goalkeeping seen on the ground in many a year kept the scoreline within respectable limits as Pavel Srnicek fought a one-man battle against the inevitable. Newcastle's cause was not helped by the loss at half-time of ex-Red Peter Beardsley, but Liverpool had been on top since the opening moments as they played with a power and pace that recalled some of their finest Championship triumphs.

Srnicek got his wake-up call after just three minutes, when he was forced to deny Fowler at close range, before doing well to keep out fierce efforts from Walters and Redknapp. The latter man was at the heart of all Liverpool's best work and ran the game with a superb passing display that levered open the visitors' defence with ominous regularity.

And it was Redknapp who played a crucial part in the opening goal. This time the visiting 'keeper turned aside a Walters drive, only for Redknapp to shoot against a post and Fowler to net the rebound.

With Liverpool rampant, Darren Peacock fluffed a back-pass to allow Fowler to round Srnicek and cross for Rush to score, and only two more stops from the Czech 'keeper stopped Fowler doubling the score in a game that proved a stark reminder of the perils of writing off Liverpool FC.

LIVERPOOL 2
NEWCASTLE UTD 0 (ht 0–0)

Venue:
Anfield

Att:
39,300

Liverpool:
James, Scales, Ruddock, Babb, Jones, McManaman, Redknapp, Barnes, Walters (Thomas 76), Fowler, Rush. (Subs not used: Molby, Warner.)

Newcastle United:
Srnicek, Hottiger, Peacock, Howey, Beresford, Gillespie, Venison, Lee, Fox (Bracewell 83), Kitson, Beardsley (Watson 46). (Sub not used: Hooper.)

Goals: Fowler (57), Rush (62)

Referee: Referee: P. Jones (Loughborough)

Jamie Redknapp was at his brilliant best as he helped the Reds to a 2–0 win against Newcastle

LIVERPOOL 2
MANCHESTER UNITED 0

Earlier in the season, Liverpool had enjoyed the better of a 2–2 draw with Manchester United, only for their performance to be overshadowed by the media hysteria that surrounded Eric Cantona's return from suspension. When the two teams met at Anfield a week before Christmas, the Reds made sure there was to be no repeat.

During the previous month – in which they went seven games without a win – Liverpool had been accused of lacking passion. No one could lay that charge against them here as they married intense commitment to some excellent football to brush United aside. Roy Evans chose the highest-profile game of the year to carry out a tactical experiment, switching Rob Jones to the left flank to allow Irishman Jason McAteer to move out to his favoured position on the right. The switch worked to perfection, with both men raiding dangerously throughout and Jones engineering an 11th-minute opening squandered by Fowler's mistimed header.

However, there were to be plenty more where that one came from and although Fowler ended up with another brace, it would not have flattered Liverpool if both he and Stan Collymore had hit hat-tricks. The former Forest star enjoyed his best game since his summer move to Anfield and was denied a goal only by the post and Peter Schmeichel.

The key to Liverpool's domination was the selection of Michael Thomas in the centre of midfield, where his play was of the highest order throughout. Yet despite having the upper hand, the home team looked worryingly likely to be held goalless until the interval. Until, that is, with 44 minutes gone, Fowler stepped up to swing a magnificent free kick around the wall into the top corner of the Kop goal, much to the surprise of Schmeichel and the glee of the Reds fans gathered behind his goal.

Liverpool continued to carry the game to United in the second half with more breathtaking skill and speed, but with Schmeichel continuing to keep Collymore out, and the visiting attackers having a couple of moments at the other end, fears of a late equalizer began to grow.

However, with three minutes to go Thomas and McManaman took play the length of the field before the latter fed the rapidly approaching Fowler, who checked inside David Beckham's desperate dive and coolly beat Schmeichel to seal the sweetest of victories for the Reds.

**LIVERPOOL 2
MANCHESTER UTD 0 (ht 1–0)**

Venue:
 Anfield

Att:
 40,546

Liverpool:
 James, Wright, Scales, Harkness, McAteer, McManaman, Thomas, Barnes, Jones, Collymore, Fowler. (Subs not used: Kennedy, Matteo, Warner.)

Manchester United:
 Schmeichel, G Neville, Bruce, May, Irwin, Beckham, McClair, Sharpe, Giggs, Cantona, Cole (Scholes, 52). (Subs not used: P Neville, Pilkington.)

Goals: Fowler (44, 87)

Referee: G Poll (Berkhampsted)

Robbie Fowler and Steve Harkness celebrate after the Fowler's second goal against Manchester United rounded off a superb team performance

FA Premiership
1 January 1996
LIVERPOOL 4
NOTTINGHAM FOREST 2

The Nottingham Forest fans came to Anfield not to praise Stan Collymore but to bury him. Collymore had left the City Ground for Anfield amid much ill-feeling and was the target for non-stop abuse from the visiting supporters. By the final whistle he had proved his point in the most emphatic manner possible while his team as a whole had bounced back from a shocking start to reassert their credentials as the best footballing side in England.

Forest went ahead after just 12 minutes, when McManaman lost out to Scouser Paul McGregor. The ball went via boyhood Liverpool fan Ian Woan to Steve Stone, who scored with a confident shot. The visiting contingent raised an equally loud cheer when Collymore headed over soon after, before McGregor and Woan combined again, the latter scoring at the near post from the former's low cross.

Liverpool had been caught napping but they woke up just after the half-hour to transform the afternoon. Big Stan Collymore suddenly decided to unveil a hitherto-unknown talent as a provider as well as a finisher when he popped up on the left to cross for Fowler to score at the near post.

There was now no stopping the Reds – and the forward partnership that had finally clicked. Crossley saved magnificently from Fowler but was helpless as Liverpool conjured up a neat replica of their opening goal to draw level by the break. The half-time interval was the only respite Forest were given as Collymore shot inches wide immediately after the resumption and went on to kill off his old team's hopes in style. Just past the hour, Crossley

---

LIVERPOOL 4
NOTTS. FOREST 2 (ht 2–2)

Venue:
   Anfield
Att:
   39,300
Liverpool:
   James, Scales, Harkness, Babb, McAteer, McManaman, Thomas, Barnes, Jones, Collymore, Fowler. Subs not used: Clough, Pears, Kennedy.
Nottingham Forest:
   Crossley, Lyttle, Cooper, Chettle, Pearce, McGregor (Roy, 73), Stone, Bart-Williams, Haaland, Woan, Campbell. (Subs not used: Phillips, Silenzi.)
Goals: Stone (12), Woan (17), Fowler (31, 40), Collymore (61), Cooper (o.g. 87)
Referee: Referee: P Alcock (Redhill)

Stan Collymore gets a hug from team-mate Robbie Fowler after Stan scored against his old club

Stan Collymore scores the most vital goal of his career as Newcastle lose out in the 91st minute

and Steve Chettle hesitated to allow their former colleague to nip between them and joyfully steer the ball into an empty net. And to add final insult to injury, Collymore's late cross forced Colin Cooper into putting through his own goal. A point hadmost certainly been proved.

FA Premiership
4 April 1996
LIVERPOOL 4
NEWCASTLE UNITED 3

Liverpool's 1977 European Cup win over St Etienne is the most famous night in Anfield's history, but there can rarely have been a more astonishing one than this. Twice Newcastle United went ahead, and twice Liverpool –who led early – came back and snatched victory right at the death.

The Reds struck first after just 97 seconds, Jamie Redknapp picking out Stan Collymore with a perfect pass down the left. When he crossed to the far post, Robbie Fowler outjumped his opponents to head downwards into the net. Newcastle picked up the gauntlet and responded in scintillating style to equalize within the quarter-hour. Les Ferdinand put the Geordies level with a fierce finish after Faustino Asprilla's skill had taken him past Neil Ruddock. David Ginola then ran clear to finish Ferdinand's pass.

The talents of Asprilla and Ginola could have extended their team's lead before half-time, but they were less effective after the break as McAteer and Ruddock

---

LIVERPOOL 4
NEWCASTLE UTD 3 (ht 1–2)

Venue:
Anfield

Att:
40,702

Liverpool:
James, Wright (Harkness 46), Scales, Ruddock, McAteer, Redknapp, Barnes, McManaman, Jones (Rush 85), Collymore, Fowler. Sub not used: Warner.

Newcastle United:
Srnicek, Watson, Howey (Peacock 82), Albert, Beresford, Beardsley, Lee, Batty, Ginola, Ferdinand, Asprilla. Subs not used: Clark, Gillespie.

Goals: Fowler (1, 54), Ferdinand (9), Ginola (14), Asprilla (56), Collymore (66, 91)

Referee: M Reed (Birmingham)

It's the same old faces and the same old scoreline for Newcastle as the two teams once again conspire to produce a sublime match. Here Robbie Fowler scores the first of his two goals on the night

got to grips with them. For Liverpool, McManaman enjoyed an inspired evening and his non-stop running eventually turned the game the home team's way.

He twice tested Srnicek before hitting a square ball along the edge of the box that Fowler hammered in to make it 2–2. But within two minutes, Newcastle were back in front: Lee fed Asprilla behind the Liverpool back line and he made no mistake against James. Both teams had now abandoned all thoughts of defending and chance followed chance at both ends before Liverpool equalized a second time when Collymore converted McAteer's cross.

Yet amid such an orgy of frenzied attack, it was ironic that the Reds' winner should come from a final moment of calm and composure. With a minute of injury time gone and the final whistle only seconds away, Rush found Barnes inside the box. Instead of swinging a hopeful boot goalwards, the wily old stager saw Collymore arriving on his left, held the ball up and then rolled it into his path for the big striker to lash in at the near post. Both managers afterwards bemoaned the standard of defending, but no one could deny that Anfield had just witnessed an attacking classic.

FA Premiership
10 March 1997
LIVERPOOL 4
NEWCASTLE UNITED 3

For the second year running, Liverpool and Newcastle United produced a magnificent 4–3 Anfield thriller decided by a goal scored deep into injury time. But this time they arrived at the same result via an entirely different route.

Whereas the previous season both sides had matched each other attack for attack, in this action replay Liverpool were for the most part playing on an entirely different plane to their Championship rivals. For more than an hour they overwhelmed Newcastle with an unstoppable blend of skill and determination before suffering a remarkable collapse, followed by an even more incredible resurrection.

With Alan Shearer injured and Les Ferdinand fit enough only to make the bench, new Magpies' boss Kenny Dalglish opted for a defensive formation that allowed Liverpool to dominate the opening stages, albeit without creating too much of a threat to the visitors' goal. Then suddenly the Reds caught fire and scored twice in two minutes at the start of a purple patch that threatened total humiliation for the visitors.

Carved open first by a McAteer cross that Fowler dummied for McManaman to curl in from 16 yards, and then by McManaman's pass to Fowler, whose shot rebounded from an upright for Berger to polish off, the Magpies were in such disarray that one fan emerged from the stand to throw his shirt at Dalglish. Liverpool were now tearing them apart at will, and it was no surprise when Redknapp's world-class pass freed Fowler to put his team 3–0 up just before the interval.

Dalglish gambled on Ferdinand, who lasted only ten minutes, and Ginola at half-time, but the action remained at the visitors' end, where Shaka Hislop did well to deny Bjornebye and Barnes. And when Newcastle did get back in the game it was through Liverpool's accidents rather than their own design. James, previously little more than a spectator, was caught napping by Keith Gillespie's 70th-minute drive and allowed the Magpies' first shot of the game to squeeze past him and into the net. That appeared to be a minor hiccup until everything went pear-shaped in the final three minutes.

A mistake by Redknapp, followed by brilliantly skilful moves from Ginola and Asprilla, saw the Colombian flick the Frenchman's pass over the impetuous James. Then the Liverpool 'keeper's nightmare continued as he missed a loose ball that Warren Barton tucked away to make it 3–3.

With that, many home fans began filing out in disgust, only for Fowler to pop up in injury time and grab his team's just desserts by crashing in a header from Bjornebye's perfect cross. What will they come up with next time?

**LIVERPOOL 4
NEWCASTLE UTD 3 (ht 3–2)**

Venue:
Anfield

Att:
40,751

Liverpool:
James, Kvarme, Wright, Matteo, McAteer, Redknapp, Barnes, Bjornebye, McManaman, Berger, Fowler. (Subs not used: Collymore, Harkness, Warner, Ruddock, Kennedy.)

Newcastle United:
Hislop, Watson, Peacock, Albert, Elliott, Gillespie, Batty, Barton, Clark (Ginola 46), Beardsley (Ferdinand 46 [Crawford 55]), Asprilla. (Subs not used: Srnicek, Beresford.)

Goals: McManaman (29), Berger (30), Fowler (42, 90), Gillespie (70), Asprilla (87), Barton (88)

Referee: D Elleray (Harrow)

Chapter 10
This is Anfield

Few English football grounds are architectural masterpieces, but they are brimming with history. Anfield holds more triumphant memories than almost any other soccer stadium in the world

The story of Anfield

ANFIELD, the world-famous home of Liverpool FC, celebrated its centenary some six years before its occupiers. For the ground's first tennants were actually bitter rivals Everton, until a row over rent saw them move to Goodison Park and Liverpool established to take their place.

The original site consisted of two fields belonging to brewers John and Joseph Orrell, one of which covered the present-day Main Stand car-park while the other — originally a cricket-pitch — became the playing surface of the team. Promotion to the top flight in 1895 prompted the club to build Anfield's first landmark, the Main Stand, whose red-and-white mock-Tudor gable and ornate ironwork were to last until the present structure replaced it almost 80 years later. That stand could hold 3,000 spectators, and the ground's

Constant development has made Anfield one of the most modern football grounds in the world

covered capacity was increased again in 1903 when a timber-and-corrugated-iron construction was assembled at the Anfield Road end. Then, in 1906, the fans who had cheered Liverpool to their second Championship were rewarded with a new bank to stand on at the Walton Breck Road end of the ground. That modest accomodation was christened the Spion Kop, and would eventually become the most famous vantage-point in football. At about the same time as the Kop was born a third stand was built, this time on Kemlyn Road, with a barrel-shaped roof and an uncovered paddock at the front.

The next major changes occured in the 1920s, as Liverpool rose again to the status of English champions. In 1928 the Kop was extended to hold 30,000 people under an enormous roof. It was by far the largest covered terrace in the country, and would remain much the same until its eventual demise in 1994. One piece of Kop

history lives on, however, in the flagpole that still stands by the Kemlyn Road corner of the stand. It was originally a topmast from the steamship Great Eastern, one of the world's first iron ships, which was broken up on the Mersey. The mast was rescued by the club and dragged up Everton Valley to rise again next to the revamped Spion Kop.

The memorial to the Hillsborough victims

Anfield then remained little-changed until well after the Second World War. Floodlights came at a cost of £12,000 in 1957 and were switched on at a special inaugural match against Everton, which the Reds won 3—2. The 1960s brought fresh success and more development work. A £350,000 cantilever stand with a capacity of 6,700 replaced the original Kemlyn Road enclosure in 1963, and two years later FA Cup triumph was followed by the building of a covered terrace at the Anfield Road end. The present Main Stand was completed in 1973 and the original floodlights were replaced by a new set, mounted along the roofs of the side stands, at a cost almost ten times that of the originals. The Main Stand paddock was equipped with seating during the summer of 1980, at the same time as undersoil heating and a pitch sprinkler system were installed, and the Anfield Road end followed suit soon after. The Shankly Gates, an 18-foot-tall, wrought-iron memorial to the great manager, bearing the legend "You'll Never Walk Alone" and costing £15,000, were erected in 1982 around the first anniversary of his death.

Little more then happened for a decade, albeit not by the club's choice. In 1978 they were offered the chance to buy 72 houses in the streets on the Kemlyn Road side of the stadium. No plans for development existed at that time, but the Reds decided to purchase the properties in case they needed to expand in the future. By 1980, with increasing success being matched by rising attendances, they drew up plans for a 4,000-seat second tier on the Kemlyn Road stand and began buying up the remaining houses in the street to make way for the extension and an accompanying car park. Within a year, every house in the street had been bought, with one exception. Nora and Jane Mason, elderly sisters living at Number 26, declined all offers to persuade them to leave. Liverpool demolished the entire street, save the Mason's house and a bricked-up dwelling shoring up either side of their home, and for years fans arriving at the ground were greeted by the strange sight of a single slice of terrace marooned amid the stadium approach. In February 1991 the sisters finally agreed to leave and building work began on the Kemlyn Road's second tier.

The £8 million stand includes Anfield's first executive boxes and has a capacity of almost 12,000. Completed at the end of the club's 100th anniversary year it was renamed the Centenary Stand and opened by UEFA president Lennart Johansson in September 1992. Kemlyn Road no longer exists.

Anfield's next and most controversial change was the redevelopment of the Spion Kop, in the light of Lord Justice Taylor's report into the Hillsborough dis-

The world-famous Spion Kop crowd in 1970. Named after a Boer War battle, the terrace held 30,000

aster which demanded the phasing-out of all terracing. The first ground changes to follow the 1989 FA Cup semi-final tragedy were the removal of the fencing at the front of the Kop — erected in 1977 to discourage (rare) pitch invasions — and the creation of the Hillsborough memorial alongside the Shankly gates. But the most far-reaching was the demolition of football's most famous terrace and its replacement with a new £7 million grandstand holding more than 12,000 spectators. The bulldozers moved in at the end of the 1993—94 season and the new Kop Grandstand opened the following year. The changes made to the ground saw it named as a European Championship venue in 1996, and the Kop now holds the souvenir shop, ticket office and club museum but, to the disappointment of the fans, is dominated by a fast-food restaurant.

That conversion reduced Anfield's capacity to just over 41,000, and with every match a sell-out the summer of 1997 saw building work commence at the Anfield Road end, to add a second tier which would boost full-house numbers to more than 45,000. A Shankly statue was erected outside the Kop at the start of the 1997—98 season and, as the Anfield Road extension headed for completion, the club's thoughts were already turning to new means of meeting a demand that continued to soar. The Main Stand is the only part of the ground where supporting pillars still obstruct some spectators' views. A new, cantilevered Main Stand roof is the logical next step in stadium development and could also create room to take capacity up to 50,000, securing Anfield's position as the second-largest club ground in the country.

Having finally abandoned the idea of building a 67,000-capacity out-of-town stadium in 1990, Liverpool know Anfield is likely to be overtaken in size by other club's proposed new grounds. But they are safe in the knowledge that their own home will rarely be anything less than packed to the rafters, and that the Liverpool team will always be inspired by the unique Anfield atmosphere.

The Spion Kop

"AS rich and mystifying a popular culture as on any South Seas island."

That was how Anfield's Spion Kop was described in a BBC Panorama documentary investigating its unique character, as Liverpool won the League in April 1964. Or, as reporter Richard Dimbleby put it: "Football worship here amounts to fanaticism".

Incongruous though the image may be of a heavyweight intellectual conducting a sociological discussion about a football crowd, the programme was correct in identifying the legend of the Kop as a human rather than physical phenomenon. It was, in its time, the largest covered terrace in English football, but it was the people who congregated beneath its cavernous roof that made it the most famous vantage-point in the entire game.

The terrace began life as a cinder mound built at the Walton Breck Road end of the Anfield ground following the Championship success of 1906, and was christened the Spion Kop soon after by Ernest Edwards, sports editor of the Liverpool Daily Post and Echo, in tribute to the many local men who died in a Boer War battle trying to capture a South African hill of the same name in January 1900. Concrete terracing and a roof erected in 1928 expanded the Kop to hold 30,000 spectators and it remained more or less unchanged for the remaining 60-odd years of its life. It changed little on the outside either, where the stilted, brick and cream plaster exterior loomed over the surrounding neighbourhood in a manner suggesting anything but a temple to the footballing arts.

But it was the colourful sights and the cacophony of noise found inside the giant structure, rather than any great architectural merit in the terrace itself, that brought the Kop worldwide fame and admiration. The origins of chanting football crowds remain unclear, although the patrons of the Kop were among the pioneers of vocal support, and by the start of the post-war period record signing Albert Stubbins found the welcome his new team received on emerging from the tunnel deafening, even in comparison to the vociferous North-East crowds with which he had grown up. "The Kop sound was the Number One," the striker said; "no doubt about it."

Number One it may have been, but it wasn't until the 1960s that the crowd enjoyed a celebrity status almost on a par with the players themselves. Liverpool burst back into the first division in 1962 and the Kop imposed itself on the national consciousness in equally spectacular fashion. Opponents in Division Two had become familiar with the all-singing, all-dancing, swaying, steaming, raucous body of fans as they fell under the spell of Bill Shankly's runaway title winners the previous season. It would not be long before the entire country did likewise.

The '60s proved a golden age for Merseyside, with the docks booming, the local economy buoyant, The Beatles and a whole trail of Merseybeat groups dominating the pop charts, and Liverpudlian comedians apparently ubiquitous over the airwaves. Even the Prime Minister was a local MP. And just as the world had heard nothing like The Beatles before, they had heard or seen nothing like the Kop either, when the Reds' Championship win of 1963—64 brought it to public attention. As well as their very own Poor Scouser Tommy, the Kopites sang She Loves You, altered the chorus of Yellow Submarine to read "We All Live in a Red and White Kop" and that of Let's Go to salute St John instead. Most famously of all, they adopted You'll Never Walk Alone as their theme song, singing it slowly and movingly, scarves held aloft, before every kick-off and in every moment of celebration in the club's modern history. Television carried the spectacle around the world for the next 30 years, where it captured the imagination of football fans to such a degree that the weekend after the Hillsborough disaster of 1989, a full-house at Milan's great San Siro sang a pitch-perfect You'll Never Walk Alone in tribute to the dead.

But just as impressive as the Kop's repertoire of singing, chanting, joking and hand-clapping was the timing and apparent spontaneity of it all. Rumours abounded of Kop conductors and organised singing, but the reality was more likely to be that the efforts of the hard-core central portion of the terrace were picked up and joined in with so quickly by the rest of the crowd that the mass singing appeared instinctive. The humour, however, whether collective or individual, was certainly spontaneous; and on occasion even more entertaining than the game itself. But while the wit on the terrace could be sharp and sophisticated, conditions remained primitive. The number of crash barriers was increased over time and capacity eventually reduced, but the crowd was generally packed enough for the ecstasy of a Liverpool goal to send spectators cascading down the concrete steps to end up yards away from their original positions, and for small boys to be casually lobbed around like beach-balls without fear for their safety. For the toilets, of course, the word "primitive" would have been a compliment, and for years were considered by many not to be worth wading through the masses to use. Those standing in front were soon the ones doing the wading.

The Kop's fame continued long after that of its home city — and the fortunes of its team — had begun to decline at the start of the '70s, but the crowd took on a different form. While Liverpool's football bounced back quickly, the port itself did not, and the relative innocence and optimism that characterised the Kop in the previous decade was replaced by a mood of defiance towards the rest of the country, particularly during the recession of the early '80s that decimated an already-reeling community. The message was that Liverpool might be economically and politically abandoned, but its football could not be ignored.

With its sea of scarves, and the red-and-white chequered flags which were the standards borne across Europe on Liverpool's long march to Continental success, the Kop retained its colour and spectacle, but was increasingly accused of having grown blasé in the face of relentless success and of being neither as funny nor as sporting as it had been in its swinging heyday. That may have been true to some degree, but as in the '60s, the Spion Kop of the '70s and '80s reflected the environment around it. Of course it had its less desirable qualities, but rarely led the world in them. It may have been infected by the bleaker, blacker mood that was seeping through society, but was still just about the only terrace to applaud visiting goalkeepers emerging from the tunnel to defend its goal. It is difficult to imagine more genuinely ecstatic scenes than those that greeted some of the successes of the 1980s, whether it be those that saw the winning of the double or followed the epic goals that became the Reds' stock-in-trade in the title win of 1987—88. Blasé is not the word. Even Arsenal's last-kick championship win of 1989 was given a sportingly healthy ovation.

However, by the time that league decider was played, all terraces were on their way out after the disaster of Hillsborough. The Kop's capacity was gradually reduced to the 16,480 that bade it an emotional farewell on April 30, 1994. A huge new Kop grand-

Anfield's emotional farewell to the terraced Kop was televised live around the world in 1994

stand swiftly took its place and although, like every all-seated ground in the country, the new Anfield may not be quite as atmospheric as the original, the inhabitants of the Spion Kop Mark Two have proved they can still put on a show worthy of their standing predecessors. It is not the bricks and mortar of the Anfield home end that is still marvelled at the world over, but the fervour of the support it houses. In the words of the song: "We are the famous, the famous Kopites."

Some Celebrity Reds

CELEBRITY footballers may be more common than celebrity fans in the image-conscious game of the 1990s, but Liverpool have always had their fair share of well-known followers.

The Reds rose to the top of the English game during the 1960s, at the same time that Merseyside pop groups and comedians were also conquering the world of showbiz. The city's most famous exports, The Beatles, always remained diplomatically coy about their footballing allegiances, but it was a happy coincidence that Gerry Marsden, whose chart-topping version of You'll Never Walk Alone was adopted as the Kop's theme song during that decade, was a confirmed Red long before he could count on a royalty come five to three on every other Saturday afternoon.

Plenty of other stars of the '60s were proud to shout for Liverpool, although in later years the Kop was more likely to be embarrassed by television's regular trotting-out of celebrity Reds such as Cilla Black and Jimmy Tarbuck, long after they had decamped to Berkshire. Tarby was always a welcome visitor to the dressing-room, but his 1983 gig in support of Margaret Thatcher probably made him less so on the Anfield terraces. Comedian Stan Boardman escaped a little more lightly, perhaps because he actually played for Liverpool reserves for a spell.

The Reds have always drawn a proportion of their players from the huge constituency of the Kop, notably Phil Thompson, Tommy Smith, David Fairclough, Jimmy Case, Sammy Lee and Ian Callaghan during the '60s and '70s. In recent times, Liverpool's local heroes have tended to be boyhood Evertonians, but among the current crop Rob Jones and Jason McAteer are lifelong Reds.

During the 1980s, celebrity Reds were fewer and farther between as Liverpool's decline made less of a virtue of its citizenship. Top kids' TV presenter Johnny

Power to the Reds ! 'Sporty' Spice Girl Mel Chisholm is a proud Liverpool fanatic

Ball was an Anfield fan, while Brookside creator Phil Redmond and playwrights Alan Bleasdale and Willy Russell kept the faith, along with Echo and the Bunnymen frontman Ian McCulloch and Radio One's finest DJ, John Peel, who delighted in presenting Top of the Pops wearing a sweater detailing every one of Liverpool's Championship successes.

The 1990s saw a resurgence in the city's music scene, with many of the best new bands having grown up on the Anfield successes of the 1970s and early '80s. Members of Cast and Space and the Lightning Seeds' Ian Broudie are all big Reds fans and, from further afield, wall-to-wall coverage of the Spice Girls regularly features Mel C, or 'Sporty' Spice as she's better known, cavorting in the latest Liverpool kit.

But one man will always remain the most popular of all Kopites. For after his retirement in 1974, Bill Shankly actually stood on the terrace whose fanaticism had raised him to the status of a footballing demi-god. Although his gesture was partly directed at the club board's failure to ask him to join them, he truly felt at home there. The inhabitants of the Kop could have desired no greater tribute.

Chapter 11

The Merseyside Derby

The annual meetings between Liverpool and Everton are among the most famous fixtures in world football. Passionate, tension-riven affairs both on and off the field, the games temporarily divide families and friends, and although the rivalry is not as friendly as popular legend has it, the still common sight of cars heading for the ground sporting the colours of both teams would be unheard of in almost any other city.

The first league derby was played at Goodison Park on 13 October 1894, and 44,000 spectators saw the Blues win 3–0 in a full–blooded encounter that set the tone of committed fervour that would characterise the next century of meetings. Everton dominated the earlier period – going unbeaten in 19 successive derbies at the start of the century – while Liverpool enjoyed their turn on top in the post–war period, stringing a seven–year, 13-league game unbeaten run together in the fixture during the 1970s. At the end of the 1996–97 season, Liverpool had 56 league victories to their credit and Everton 52, with a further 48 games drawn.

Tension and the high stakes of local pride mean that the derby is rarely a feast of open, flowing football, but many of the encounters in league and cup competition still stand out.

Liverpool's biggest win – a 6–0 Anfield triumph – came before the war, but modern fans still celebrate the 5–0 win at Goodison in 1982 that saw Ian Rush score four times. Other classic league encounters include a pair of 3–2 victories from 1970 and 1985. In the earlier game, Liverpool trailed 2–0 at Anfield with only 21 minutes to play in what was only striker John Toshack's second game for the club. But the giant Welshman earned instant hero status by turning the game on its head as the Reds fought back to win 3–2. Toshack scored the equaliser himself and then won the flick-on from which full-back Chris Lawler scored a late winner at the far post.

A decade and a half later, Goodison saw one of the classic derbies – and one of Kenny Dalglish's finest Liverpool performances: The great Scot scored the fastest goal of his career to put the Reds ahead in just 20 seconds before Rush and Steve McMahon gave the visitors a 3–0 half-time lead. But Everton fought back to 3–2 and with Gary Lineker hitting the crossbar, Liverpool held out for a memorable victory.

That 1985–86 season ended with the Reds beating the Blues at Wembley to clinch the League and FA Cup double in another enthralling encounter in which Liverpool came from behind to win 3–1. The two teams had first met beneath the twin towers in the

1984 League Cup Final, won by a Graeme Souness goal in a replay, but their most exciting knockout clashes came in the FA Cup. A Bob Paisley lob and a Billy Liddell winner gave Liverpool victory in the 1950 semi–final, and the Reds repeated the dose in 1977 after a replay.

The 1989 post-Hillsborough final produced one of the most dramatic meetings between the teams as John Aldridge's early goal was cancelled out with almost the last kick of normal time before the Reds rallied to win 3–2 in the extra half hour. But the most astonishing cup-tie the two teams played came in the fifth round of the 1991 competition, in what proved to be Kenny Dalglish's last game in charge. Liverpool led four times in the game's 120 minutes, but were pegged back on each occasion in a game where chances flowed non-stop at either end.

Ian Rush – A Merseyside Derby Legend

To the old adage that the only certainties of this world are death and taxes, football fans might like to add the likelihood that Ian Rush would score against Everton.

For more than 15 years the Liverpool legend tortured the Reds' chief rivals with a relentless barrage of goals. Rush struck more times against the team he supported as a boy than anyone else in derby history,

Rush and Fowler – master and apprentice

and scored more times against the Blues than he did against any other side. His final derby tally of 25 goals in 38 games shattered Dixie Dean's previous record total for the fixture.

The great Welshman started much as he intended to continue by scoring on his derby debut, helping Liverpool to a 3–1 Anfield win in November 1981. He drew a blank on his first visit to Goodison but made amends the following

season, 1982–83, when he became the only player in almost half a century to score four goals in the fixture, as Liverpool romped home 5–0 on a heaven-sent afternoon for Kopites. Rush even said afterwards: "I could have had six. I hit the bar and missed a couple of chances I should have taken."

Yet the most valuable of his derby goals was still to come. Having pipped Everton for the 1985–86 League Championship, Liverpool faced them again in the FA Cup Final. The Blues led at half-time, but two typically cool finishes from Rush gave Liverpool a 3–1 win and an historic double.

His victims must have thought they had seen the back of him when he moved to Juventus in 1987, but a year later he was back – and back in the old routine. Liverpool faced Everton again in the 1989 FA Cup final and although this time the Blues forced extra-time, Rush struck twice in the added half hour to sink them yet again.

Even in the twilight of his Anfield years he refused to let up and Liverpool's last derby win of his career was built on the foundations of another goal by Ian Rush. When he left for Leeds United in 1996, it would have been no surprise if a posse of Evertonians had insisted on escorting him to the city limits.

7 December 1992
FA Premier League
EVERTON 2
LIVERPOOL 1

Goals: 0–1 Wright (62 mins), 1–1 Johnston (63 mins), 2–1 Beardsley (85 mins)

The Merseyside derby is rarely incident-free, but the first local clash of the Premiership era took its time to ignite. Although neither side was enjoying a great season, Everton's form was so miserable that they went into the fixture as clear underdogs despite the scourge of Goodison, Ian Rush, having been ruled out by a hamstring strain.

John Barnes posed the greatest threat for Liverpool in the first half as he gave out–of–position Martin Keown a torrid time down the left, but the goalkeepers were rarely troubled before the break. Everton made an interval switch by abandoning their five-man defence to relieve the beleaguered Keown and suddenly the game burst into life with a breath-taking passage of play soon after the hour mark that yielded two goals in as many minutes.

Liverpool won a corner and when Mike Marsh floated over an inch-perfect cross, Mark Wright rose high to power a header into the net. But before the Reds could set about defending the lead, Everton were level. Straight from the restart they worked the ball to Maurice Johnston, who turned sharply and curled a left foot shot past Mike Hooper's dive.

The action switched back to the other end as Liverpool pushed on in search of another goal, only to see a John Barnes drive rebound off an upright. And then, in the dying minutes, came the final indignity, as two Anfield old boys sold by Graeme Souness combined to give Everton victory. Gary Ablett squeezed a through-ball to Peter Beardsley, and the England star rifled an instant right-footer low into the goal to settle the issue – and maybe an old score.

20 March 1993
FA Premier League
LIVERPOOL 1
EVERTON 0

Goal: 1–0 Rosenthal (91 mins)

With all hope of silverware long gone, revenge victory in the Anfield derby was the sum total of Liverpool fans' ambitions as the end of the season approached. And although the win only arrived with virtually the last kick of the game, it nonetheless tasted no less sweet for so doing.

The supporters who had already begun drifting away from what looked like a 0–0 draw were obviously unfamiliar with the work of striker Ronnie Rosenthal. The Israeli international made his name with a string of late winners that pushed Liverpool to the title in 1989–90. And he was up to his old tricks again here as a second-half substitute, coolly taking the one chance he was presented with by drilling home Rush's clever pass in front of an ecstatic Kop a full minute into injury time.

The game had not been a classic, but the goal was just reward for a second half of constant Liverpool pressure that reduced Everton to sniping on the counter attack. But the Blues had their chances too, with Stuart Barlow missing the target when well placed on three separate occasions. That apart, David James had only one routine save to make.

At the other end, however, Neville Southall needed to be at his best to deny Walters, Rush and Hutchison twice, while McManaman followed Barlow's example in squandering three presentable chances. The last of those misses saw him soon replaced by Rosenthal. Fortunately for Liverpool, the substitute made no mistake with the first opportunity that came his way.

18 September 1993
FA Premier League
EVERTON 2
LIVERPOOL 0

Goals: 1–0 Ward (27 mins), 2–0 Cottee (85 mins)

Emotions have always run high in the tension of a derby match, and have often been known to spill over into minor fisticuffs on the field. But the fact that it was two Liverpool players who were squaring up to each other after less than half an hour of this game summed up the chaos in the Anfield ranks that left them floundering throughout a nightmare afternoon that could not end quickly enough for them.

Grobbelaar and McManaman were the sparring partners in question after the goalkeeper took issue with his team-mate over the weak clearance that fell for Mark Ward to thump Everton into the lead. If only the rest of the team had shown the same fighting spirit then they might not have been so embarassingly outgunned by their city rivals. In fact, only Grobbelaar's heroics stood between the Blues and a far larger margin of victory. The 35-year-old keeper had pulled off two spectacular flying saves before Everton took the lead and only another pair of stunning interventions kept his team in touch at the break.

The early introduction of Ronnie Rosenthal's pace and purpose briefly galvanised the Reds in the second half and, after Julian Dicks drew a save from Southall, the substitute's cross almost created an equaliser for the stretching Rush. But Everton rode out the storm and sealed victory five minutes from the end when the otherwise reliable Dicks was robbed by Tony Cottee, who rounded Wright and Grobbelaar to score.

13 March 1994
FA Premier League
LIVERPOOL 2
EVERTON 1

Goals: 0–1 Watson (22 mins), 1–1 Rush (22 mins), 2–1 Fowler (44 mins)

The fortunes of Liverpool FC nosedived throughout

the first half of 1993–94 and by the time the last derby to be played in front of Anfield's terraced Kop came round they had a new manager in Roy Evans. They also had a new goalscoring hero in Robbie Fowler, although, as Everton could soon vouch, there was still plenty of life left in the old one.

At the age of 32, Ian Rush had no intention of closing his bulging account against the Blues. And Liverpool's victory in the 150th Merseyside league derby demonstrated that scoring against Everton was a striking tradition his young apprentice would be certain to uphold, as he marked his debut in the fixture with the winning goal.

The game was an exciting spectacle and whereas the previous season it was Everton who hit back immediately after conceding the lead and went on to win, this time it was Liverpool's turn. After a foul by Dicks, Preki floated in a free-kick from which Dave Watson headed the visitors into the lead. But straight from the restart, Dicks redeemed himself with a long ball that sent Rush through to score his 25th goal against his favourite opponents.

McManaman then forced a fine save out of Southall before Fowler latched on to Barnes's through-pass and finished with a precisely placed shot. Everton applied most of the pressure after the interval, but Southall had to make four fine saves as Liverpool attacked on the break. David James tipped over Peter Beagrie's deflected drive in the last minute, but it was Rush and Fowler who carried the day.

21 November 1994
FA Premier League
EVERTON 2
LIVERPOOL 0

Goals: 1–0 Ferguson (56 mins), 2–0 Rideout (89 mins)

Going into a derby as red-hot favourites is always a recipe for disaster, let alone doing so at a time when your bottom-of-the-table opponents have nowhere to go but up and are out to impress a new manager.

However, Liverpool seemed to ignore the omens when they faced Everton at Goodison in Joe Royle's first game in charge and believed the pre-match predictions that their cultured passing game would outclass their rivals' scuffling. How wrong they were, as for the second successive season they were hustled out of their stride by a side who seized the spoils by virtue

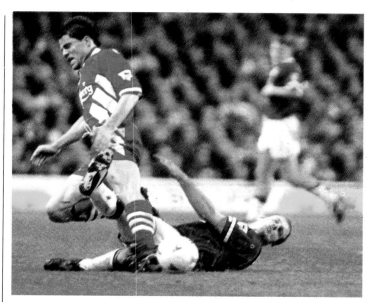

Stig Inge Bjornebye gets stuck in Merseyside style during the 2–0 defeat in November 1994

of their greater hunger for victory.

The brave Neil Ruddock excepted, Liverpool were not at the races and although they survived the first half with their goal intact and saw Southall save superbly from McManaman soon after the break, Everton's muscular grip on midfield always gave them the upper hand. And once Duncan Ferguson headed Hinchcliffe's corner past the rooted James on 56 minutes, the result was not in doubt. A last minute second goal was a luxury rather than a necessity for the Blues. James lost Hinchcliffe's cross as he collided with Ferguson and the ball fell for Rideout – who had earlier hit a post – to tap into the empty net.

Liverpool had been handing out free lessons in the art of pinpoint passing throughout the early part of the season, but at Goodison they seized up and failed to win the battle for the right to play – and paid the highest of prices for it.

24 JANUARY 1995
FA Premier League
LIVERPOOL 0
EVERTON 0

With the rough and tumble of Plan A having worked so well at Goodison Park a couple of months earlier, Everton were unlikely to switch to an expansive Plan B for the return match at Anfield, and so it proved in one of the most prosaic if uncompromising derbies in recent memory.

At least Liverpool refused to knuckle under this time, even if their opponents physical approach – which sparked an angry post-match outburst from Roy Evans – subjected them to painful punishment throughout. The Reds' boss afterwards declared himself "angry and frustrated" by Everton's destructive, strong–arm tactics and decried their "School of Science" nickname, so triggering a row with his opposite number, Joe Royle.

Everton's sole ambition appeared to be to stop everything that moved – and they weren't fussy about how they achieved it. The Blues collected four yellow cards and could have had David Burrows sent off for a second heavy foul on Fowler. They got the point they came for, although forcing a couple of late saves from the confident James was the sum total of all they could muster in attack.

Liverpool found it impossible to get their passing game going in the midfield log-jam but rolled up their sleeves to carve out several openings of their own. Bjornebye's cross forced Unsworth to head narrowly wide of his own posts before Fowler had a shot blocked by Watson and Southall parried low down from Scales. But on an evening of stodgy stalemate, a goal never really looked likely to relieve the tedium.

18 NOVEMBER 1995
FA Premier League
LIVERPOOL 1
EVERTON 2

Goals: 0–1 Kanchelskis (53 mins), 0–2 Kanchelskis (68 mins), 1–2 Fowler (89 mins)

In the previous season's derbies, Liverpool were out-fought by Everton's so-called "Dogs of War". In this meeting, however, the Reds were frustratingly out-thought and out-played by opponents who now seemed to have the Indian Sign over them.

Liverpool had lost Jamie Redknapp with a torn hamstring suffered on midweek international duty and switching Jason McAteer onto centre stage was an experiment that didn't really work as the hosts frus-tratingly passed themselves to sleep. And when they did shoot at goal, although they mustered 10 shots on target, few of their attempts extended Southall.

Rush was unlucky to have a follow-up to a Fowler effort ruled out for offside before the interval, but in the second half Liverpool added poor defending to their list of sins. Everton had decided to let their oppo-

nents have the ball in their own half and try to strike quickly on the break. The plan looked promising when Stuart forced two good saves out of James before striking a post and after the hour it brought its reward.

First, Phil Babb allowed Rideout to centre from the right for Kanchelskis to head home, and then the same defender was caught out by Limpar's crossfield pass to Kanchelskis. The Ukrainian winger ran on to dou-ble the visitors' lead. Robbie Fowler scored a close range consolation near the end but the fact that Liverpool were by then using Ruddock as a crude emergency striker said most about their sorry plight.

16 APRIL 1995
FA Premier League
EVERTON 1
LIVERPOOL 1

Goals: 1–0 Kanchelskis (18 mins), 1–1 Fowler (87 mins)

Ian Rush took his final bow in the Merseyside derby as a late Goodison substitute, but as one torturer of Evertonians hung up his thumb-screws his successor promised another decade of pain for the Blues.

Rush, the record scorer in this fixture, could not mark his farewell with a goal, but his striking succes-sor hit a deserved equaliser just three minutes from time. Robbie Fowler volleyed home the third score of his short derby career by getting on the end of Stan Collymore's inviting cross from the left to provide a just reward for an impressive second-half fightback.

The injury-hit Blues came out battling and, on a waterlogged, unforked pitch that suited their unso-phisticated hustling game, forced Liverpool into a string of errors. The slippery surface denied them two early chances but on 18 minutes, Southall's punt sailed into the visitors' penalty box, where Ebbrell skated past James for Kanchelskis to score on the rebound when his narrow-angle shot rolled against the post.

A brace of saves from James kept Liverpool in the game at half-time and after the break the Reds at last grabbed the match by the scruff of the neck. McManaman was the key to the recovery, turning on an unstoppable display down the right that threat-ened danger every time he got the ball. Collymore almost squirmed a shot past Southall from McManaman's pass and then drove a long-range effort against the crossbar before finally teeing up Fowler to score at the death.

20 NOVEMBER 1996
FA Premier League
LIVERPOOL 1
EVERTON 1

Goals: 1–0 Fowler (29 mins), 1–1 Speed (82 mins)

The first attempt to play this fixture was washed out by a ferocious pre-match downpour, and when the replay came round Liverpool were no doubt delighted at having a perfect pitch to help their bid to go top of the Premiership.

But in a game of only moderate quality, their derby jinx struck again, this time with the Reds an agonising few minutes away from victory. Liverpool had dominated the opening spell and, after losing McManaman early on with hamstring trouble, had the excellent Stig Inge Bjornebye to thank for creating the chance from which Fowler gave them the lead.

The wing–back served notice of his intent on 26 minutes when his pinpoint corner saw Mark Wright's header cleared off the line. And a few moments later, after Southall had tipped over Redknapp's sizzling 25-yarder, he got another chance to put the Blues under pressure. Watson headed Bjornebye's flag–kick straight

Jamie Redknapp celebrates Thomsen's own goal

back to him and the Norwegian unerringly picked out Fowler, who bulleted home an unmarked header.

Southall had to save twice from substitute Collymore and Barnes later shaved a post, but Liverpool lost their way in the second half. Everton had introduced Ferguson at half-time and their opponents quickly played into their hands by defending too deeply and allowing the Blues to launch a succession of long balls towards the big Scot. Pressure began to mount and after Speed ghosted in to head home Hinchcliffe's free-kick, Liverpool were grateful not to concede a winner amid several frantic late scrambles.

16 APRIL 1997
FA Premier League
EVERTON 1
LIVERPOOL 1

Goals: 0–1 Thomsen o.g. (26 mins), 1–1 Ferguson (65 mins)

Everton were languishing in relegation country by the time of the season's second derby, but they took great delight in denting Liverpool's title ambitions by extending the Reds' winless sequence in the fixture to six games.

Liverpool held the edge in a passionate encounter for more than an hour, until Ferguson rescued a point for the Blues and the match ended in controversy as Fowler and Unsworth were sent off for aiming punches at each other in the culmination of a running feud. The Everton defender's initial foul might have merited a dismissal in itself, but Fowler also paid the price for retaliating.

The committed tone of the game was set from the off when Ferguson was lucky to escape a 12-second booking for flattening derby debutant Bjorn Tore Kvarme. The classy Norwegian went on to match his opponent throughout and denied the home attack a sniff of goal until after long after Liverpool had taken the lead. Fowler and McManaman combined down the right, from where the latter crossed for Redknapp to force an own-goal out of Claus Thomsen. And Liverpool almost extended their advantage when, in a single second-half minute, Southall saved brilliantly from Redknapp and Fowler hit both post and crossbar.

The conversion of just one of those chances would have killed the game off, but Everton bounced back to equalise through Ferguson's fine shot on the turn and deny Liverpool another chance to top the League.

Chapter 12

The Records

The name of Liverpool FC is synonymous with record-breaking excellence. No other English club can come close to the Reds' total of 18 League Championships, four European Cups, two UEFA Cups, five FA Cups and five League Cups. Many of the team's most vital statistics stand as benchmarks for the entire English game.

The Merseyside club's record of 16 goals conceded in the 42 games of the 1978–79 campaign is unlikely ever to be equalled, as is their 1984 treble of League title, European Cup and League Cup. Their best points tally in the three points for a win era has been matched only by their neighbours, Everton.

But Liverpool have also been ground-breakers in areas other than the black and white of the statistics book. The history of televised football began at Anfield with the very first edition of the BBC's *Match of the Day*, when the Reds beat Arsenal 3–2 in August 1964, with Roger Hunt scoring the first goal seen on the small screen. And when colour TV arrived later in the decade, it was Anfield that ushered in another age with the screening of highlights of their 2–0 win over West Ham United in January 1967. That time it was two-goal winger Peter Thompson who was the star of the show. Anfield has seen its fair share of heroes over the years, and here are some of their club record-breaking exploits.

MOST APPEARANCES

1.	Ian Callaghan	843 (+5 as sub)
2.	Emlyn Hughes	657
3.	Ray Clemence	656
4.	Phil Neal	633 (+2)
5.	Tommy Smith	632 (+1)
6.	Ian Rush	621 (+28)
7.	Bruce Grobbelaar	610
8.	Alan Hansen	603 (+4)
9.	Chris Lawler	546
10.	Billy Liddell	537

MOST GOALS

1.	Ian Rush	338
2.	Roger Hunt	285
3.	Gordon Hodgson	240
4.	Billy Liddell	229
5.	Kenny Dalglish	168
6.	Harry Chambers	151
7.	Jack Parkinson	128
8.	Sam Raybould	127
9.	Dick Forshaw	124
10.	Ian St John	118

MISCELLANEOUS LIVERPOOL RECORDS

Fastest hat-trick

Robbie Fowler 4 mins, 33 secs, v Arsenal, 28 Aug, 1994

Other notable goalscoring feats

Kenny Dalglish is the only player to score 100 goals in both England and Scotland

Jack Balmer scored hat-tricks in three successive matches in November 1946

Most caps

Kenny Dalglish – 102 Scotland caps (55 as a Liverpool player)

Emlyn Hughes – 62 England caps (59 as a Liverpool player)

Most league goals scored in a season

Roger Hunt –	41 goals in 41 games (Div. 2), 1961–62
	31 goals in 41 games (Div. 1), 1963–64
Ian Rush –	32 goals in 41 games (Div. 1), 1983–84

Most goals scored in a season (all competitions)

Ian Rush – 48 goals in 64 games, 1983–84

MISCELLANEOUS LIVERPOOL RECORDS

Most goals scored in a season (by whole team)

106 – Div. 2, 1895–96

92 – Div. 1, 1963–64

Fewest goals conceded

16 – Div. 1, 1978–79

Most league points

68 – 1978–79 (two points for a win)

90 – 1989–90 (three points for a win)

Biggest win

11–0 v Stromgodset, European Cup Winners' Cup, September 11, 1974

Biggest defeat

1–9 v Birmingham City, Div. 2, December 11, 1954

Highest attendance

61,905 v Wolverhampton Wanderers, FA Cup 4th Round, February 2, 1952

Transfer records

Liverpool have always enjoyed a reputation for shrewd bargain buying in the transfer market, but the Reds have rarely baulked at paying top prices for top quality. And even their most expensive purchases have generally given outstanding value for money.

Transfer fees became the norm around the turn of the century and when Alf Common became the game's first £1,000 player by moving from Sunderland to Middlesbrough in 1905, Liverpool were setting their own record at £500 in buying goalkeeper Sam Hardy from Chesterfield. They got immediate value as Hardy became one of the finest keepers of his era and helped the Reds to the Championship in his very first season.

The Anfield side really stepped into the big money league in 1929, when the £8,000 it cost them to prise Tom Bradshaw away from Bury was the fourth highest fee in history. They went even further after the Second World War by paying £13,000 for Newcastle United striker Albert Stubbins – a sum that had only ever been topped once. Again the investment paid off as Stubbins's goals brought Liverpool the Championship of 1946–47.

It took only 20 years for transfer fees to go from scraping into five figures to smashing through the £100,000 barrier. Chelsea spent that in 1966 on Aston Villa's Tony Hateley – who would join Liverpool for £96,000 a year later – and Bill Shankly spent his first six figure sum on Wolves 18-year-old Alun Evans. The career of Britain's most expensive teenager was sadly blighted by injury.

By 1977, the Reds were in record-breaking mood again and had money to spend. After winning the European Cup, Kevin Keegan's move to Hamburg had netted them a record £500,000, and they paid £440,000 of that to Celtic for Kenny Dalglish. It was then the largest sum ever to change hands between two British clubs and still looks the greatest bargain the Reds ever struck. However, at the end of the decade when prices really began to rocket, Liverpool were disinclined to fuel the inflation. It was two years after Trevor Francis became the country's first £1 million player before Bob Paisley even went close to paying a seven-figure sum, when he bought Mark Lawrenson from Brighton for £900,000.

When Liverpool did break that barrier a full decade after Francis's landmark move from Birmingham to Nottingham Forest, they did so in style. Kenny Dalglish spent a club and British record £1.9 million on Newcastle's Peter Beardsley and, as with Albert Stubbins 40 years earlier, another Championship immediately followed the move.

Players rarely left Liverpool for large sums in the 1960s and '70s, but Keegan's move to Germany heralded the start of a period in which cash-rich continental clubs proved increasingly attractive. The Reds' success at home and abroad left them relatively unscathed by the exodus until Ian Rush moved to Juventus for a British record £3.2 million in 1987. Things didn't work out for him in Italy and a year later £2.8 million brought him back to Anfield.

That fee was topped by £100,000 in 1991 when Graeme Souness bought Dean Saunders from Derby, the first in a number of recent record buys to meet with only mixed success. Phil Babb's arrival in 1994 raised the benchmark to £3.75 million but he failed to establish himself in his first three seasons. And then came the club and domestic record £8.5 million paid for Stan Collymore in 1995, only to sell the misfit striker on to Aston Villa for £7 million just two frustrating years later. Yet although Collymore proved a flop, Roy Evans continued to dip into the Liverpool piggy bank and in the summer of 1997 paid nearly £5 million for Paul Ince and Karlheinz Riedle.

Year-by-year statistics – season 1992–93

	FA PREMIER LEAGUE				
Date	Team	Venue	Att	Score	Scorer
Aug 16	Nottingham F	A	20,038	0–1	
Aug 19	Sheffield U	H	33,107	2–1	Walters, Stewart
Aug 23	Arsenal	H	34,961	0–2	
Aug 25	Ipswich T	A	20,109	2–2	Walters, Molby (pen)
Aug 29	Leeds U	A	29,597	2–2	Whelan, Molby (pen)
Sep 1	Southampton	H	30,024	1–1	Wright
Sep 5	Chelsea	H	34,199	2–1	Saunders, Redknapp
Sep 12	Sheffield U	A	20,632	0–1	
Sep 19	Aston Villa	A	37,863	2–4	Walters, Rosenthal
Sep 26	Wimbledon	H	29,574	2–3	Molby (pen), McManaman
Oct 3	Sheffield W	H	35,785	1–0	Hutchison
Oct 18	Manchester U	A	33,243	2–2	Hutchison, Rush
Oct 25	Norwich C	H	36,318	4–1	Thomas, Hutchison, Burrows, Walters (pen)
Oct 31	Tottenham H	A	32,917	0–2	
Nov 7	Middlesbrough	H	34,974	4–1	Rosenthal 2, McManaman, Rush
Nov 23	QPR	A	21,056	1–0	Rosenthal
Nov 28	Crystal Palace	H	36,380	5–0	McManaman 2, Rosenthal, Hutchison
Dec 7	Everton	A	35,826	1–2	Wright
Dec 13	Blackburn R	H	43,668	2–1	Walters 2
Dec 19	Coventry C	A	19,779	1–5	Redknapp
Dec 28	Manchester C	H	43,037	1–1	Rush
Jan 9	Aston Villa	H	40,826	1–2	Barnes
Jan 16	Wimbledon	A	11,294	0–2	
Jan 31	Arsenal	A	27,580	1–0	Barnes (pen)
Feb 6	Nottingham F	H	40,463	0–0	
Feb 1	Chelsea	A	20,981	0–0	
Feb 1	Southampton	A	17,216	1–2	Hutchison
Feb 20	Ipswich T	H	36,680	0–0	
Feb 27	Sheffield W	A	33,964	1–1	Hutchison
Mar 6	Manchester U	H	44,374	1–2	Rush
Mar 10	QPR	H	30,370	1–0	Rush
Mar 13	Middlesbrough	A	22,463	2–1	Hutchison, Rush
Mar 20	Everton	H	44,619	1–0	Rosenthal
Mar 23	Crystal Palace	A	18,688	1–1	Rush
Apr 3	Blackburn R	A	15,032	1–4	Rush
Apr 10	Oldham A	H	36,129	1–0	Rush
Apr 12	Manchester C	A	28,098	1–1	Rush
Apr 17	Coventry C	H	33,328	4–0	Walters 3 (1 pen), Burrows
Apr 21	Leeds U	H	34,992	2–0	Barnes, Walters (pen)
May 1	Norwich C	A	20,610	0–1	
May 5	Oldham A	A	15,381	2–3	Rush 2
May 8	Tottenham H	H	43,385	6–2	Rush 2, Barnes 2, Harkness, Walters (pen)

Final League position: 6th

EUROPEAN CUP-WINNERS' CUP

Date	Team	Venue	Att	Score	Scorer
1st Round					
1st L Sep 16	Apollon Limassol	H	12,769	6–1	Stewart 2, Rush 4
2nd L Sep 29	Apollon Limassol	A	12,000	2–1	Rush, Hutchison
2nd Round					
1st L Oct 22	Spartak Moscow	A	55,000	2–4	Wright, McManaman
2nd L Nov 4	Spartak Moscow	H	37,993	0–2	

PLAYER RECORDS

Name	App	(Sub)	L. Goals	Other Goals
Wright	32	1	2	1 European, 1 League Cup
Nicol	32			
Rush	31	1	14	5 European, 1 FA Cup, 1 League Cup
Jones	30			
Burrows	29	1	2	
James	29			
Hutchison	27	4	7	1 European, 2 League Cup
McManaman	27	4	4	1 European, 2 League Cup
Redknapp	27	2	2	1 League Cup
Walters	26	8	11	2 League Cup
Barnes	26	1	5	
Marsh	22	6	1	3 League Cup
Stewart	21	3	1	2 European goals
Whelan	17		1	
Rosenthal	16	11	6	1 League Cup
Piechnik	15	1		
Bjornebye	11			
Harkness	9	1	1	
Molby	8	2	3	
Hooper	8	1		
Thomas	6	2	1	
Saunders	6		1	
Grobbelaar	5			
Tanner	2	2		
Kozma	0	1		

FA CUP

Date	Team	Venue	Att	Score	Scorer
3rd Round					
Jan 3	Bolton W	A	21,502	2–2	Winstanley (og), Rush
3rd Round Replay					
Jan 13	Bolton W	H	34,790	0–2	

COCA-COLA CUP

Date	Team	Venue	Att	Score	Scorer
2nd Round					
1st L Sep 22	Chesterfield	H	12,533	4–4	Rosenthal, Hutchison, Walters, Wright
2nd L Oct 6	Chesterfield	A	10,632	4–1	Hutchison, Redknapp, Walters, Rush
3rd Round					
Oct 28	Sheffield U	A	17,856	0–0	
3rd round replay					
Nov 11	Sheffield U	H	17,654	3–0	McManaman 2, Marsh (pen)
4th Round					
Dec 1	Crystal Palace	H	18,525	1–1	Marsh (pen)
4th Round replay					
Dec 16	Crystal Palace	A	16,622	1–2 (aet)	Marsh (pen)

Ronnie Whelan turns in triumph after scoring for Liverpool in the 2–2 draw with Leeds in 1992–93

Year-by-year statistics – season 1993–94

			FA PREMIER LEAGUE		
Date	**Team**	**Venue**	**Att**	**Score**	**Scorer**
Aug 14	Sheffield W	H	44,004	2–0	Clough 2
Aug 18	QPR	A	19,635	3–1	Nicol, Clough, Rush
Aug 22	Swindon T	A	17,017	5–0	Ruddock, Whelan, McManaman 2, Marsh
Aug 25	Tottenham H	H	42,456	1–2	Clough
Aug 28	Leeds U	H	44,068	2–0	Molby, Rush
Sep 1	Coventry C	A	16,740	0–1	
Sep 12	Blackburn R	H	37,355	0–1	
Sep 18	Everton	A	38,157	0–2	
Sep 25	Chelsea	A	31,271	0–1	
Oct 2	Arsenal	H	42,750	0–0	
Oct 16	Oldham A	H	32,661	2–1	Fowler, Barlow (og)
Oct 23	Manchester C	A	30,403	1–1	Rush
Oct 30	Southampton	H	32,818	4–2	Rush, Fowler 3
Nov 6	West Ham U	H	42,254	2–0	Clough, Martin (og)
Nov 21	Newcastle U	A	36,374	0–3	
Nov 28	Aston Villa	H	30,403	2–1	Redknapp, Fowler
Dec 4	Sheffield W	A	32,818	1–3	Fowler
Dec 8	QPR	H	24,561	3–2	Molby (pen), Barnes, Rush
Dec 11	Swindon T	H	32,739	2–2	Barnes, Wright
Dec 18	Tottenham H	A	31,394	3–3	Redknapp, Fowler 2
Dec 26	Sheffield U	A	22,932	0–0	
Dec 28	Wimbledon	H	32,232	1–1	Scales (og)
Jan 1	Ipswich	A	22,355	2–1	Ruddock, Rush
Jan 4	Manchester U	H	42,795	3–3	Clough 2, Ruddock
Jan 15	Oldham A	A	14,573	3–0	Dicks, Redknapp, Fowler
Jan 22	Manchester C	H	41,872	2–1	Rush 2
Feb 5	Norwich C	A	19,746	2–2	Barnes, Culverhouse (og)
Feb 14	Southampton	A	18,306	2–4	Dicks (pen), Rush
Feb 19	Leeds U	A	40,053	0–2	
Feb 26	Coventry C	H	38,547	1–0	Rush
Mar 5	Blackburn R	A	20,831	0–2	
Mar 13	Everton	H	44,281	2–1	Rush, Fowler
Mar 19	Chelsea	H	38,629	2–1	Rush, Burley (og)
Mar 26	Arsenal	A	35,556	0–1	
Mar 30	Manchester U	A	44,751	0–1	
Apr 2	Sheffield U	H	36,642	1–2	Rush
Apr 4	Wimbledon	A	13,819	1–1	Redknapp
Apr 9	Ipswich T	H	30,485	1–0	Dicks (pen)
Apr 16	Newcastle U	H	44,601	0–2	
Apr 23	West Ham U	A	26,096	2–1	Rush, Fowler
Apr 30	Norwich C	H	44,339	0–1	
May 7	Aston Villa	A	45,347	1–2	Fowler

Final League position: 8th

FA CUP

Date	Team	Venue	Att	Score	Scorer
3rd Round					
Jan 19	Bristol C	A	21,718	1–1	Rush
3rd Round Replay					
Jan 25	Bristol C	H	36,720	0–1	

COCA-COLA CUP

Date	Team	Venue	Att	Score	Scorer
2nd Round					
1st L Sep 22	Fulham	A	13,599	3–1	Clough, Rush, Fowler
2nd L Oct 5	Fulham	H	12,541	5–0	Fowler 5
3rd Round					
Oct 27	Ipswich T	H	19,058	3–2	Rush 3
4th Round					
Dec 1	Wimbledon	H	19,290	1–1	Molby (pen)
4th Round replay (Wimbledon won 4–3 on penalties)					
Dec 14	Wimbledon	A	11,343	2–2(aet)	Ruddock, Segars (og)

PLAYER RECORDS

Name	App	(Sub)	L. Goals	Other Goals
Rush	41		13	1 FA Cup, 4 League Cup
Ruddock	39		3	1 League Cup
Jones	31		1	
Redknapp	29	6	4	
McManaman	29	1	2	
Grobbelaar	29			
Nicol	27	4	1	
Fowler	27	1	12	6 League Cup
Clough	25	1	7	1 League Cup
Barnes	24	2	3	
Dicks	24		3	
Whelan	23		1	
James	13	1		
Molby	11		2	1 League Cup
Matteo	11			
Harkness	10			
Walters	7	10		
Stewart	7		1	
Hutchison	6		5	
Bjornebye	6		3	
Burrows	3		1	
Thomas	1	6		
Piechnik	1			
Rosenthal	0	3		
Marsh	0	2	1	

Steve McManaman celebrates his first goal for Liverpool in the 1993 5–0 thrashing of Swindon

Year-by-year statistics – season 1994–95

	FA PREMIER LEAGUE				
Date	Team	Venue	Att	Score	Scorer
Aug 20	Crystal Palace	A	18,084	6–1	Molby (pen), McManaman 2, Fowler, Rush 2
Aug 28	Arsenal	H	30,017	3–0	Fowler 3
Aug 31	Southampton	A	15,190	2–0	Fowler, Barnes
Sep 10	West Ham U	H	30,907	0–0	
Sep 17	Manchester U	A	43,740	0–2	
Sep 24	Newcastle U	A	34,435	1–1	Rush
Oct 1	Sheffield W	H	31,493	4–1	McManaman 2, Walker (og), Rush
Oct 8	Aston Villa	H	32,158	3–2	Ruddock, Fowler 2
Oct 15	Blackburn R	A	30,263	2–3	Fowler, Barnes
Oct 22	Wimbledon	H	31,139	3–0	McManaman, Fowler, Barnes
Oct 29	Ipswich T	A	22,379	3–1	Barnes, Fowler 2
Oct 31	QPR	A	18,295	1–2	Barnes
Nov 5	Nottingham F	H	33,329	1–0	Fowler
Nov 9	Chelsea	H	32,885	3–1	Fowler 2, Ruddock
Nov 21	Everton	A	39,886	0–2	
Nov 26	Tottenham H	H	35,007	1–1	Fowler (pen)
Dec 3	Coventry C	A	21,032	1–1	Rush
Dec 11	Crystal Palace	H	30,972	0–0	
Dec 18	Chelsea	A	27,050	0–0	
Dec 26	Leicester C	A	21,393	2–1	Fowler (pen), Rush
Dec 28	Manchester C	H	38,122	2–0	Phelan (og), Fowler
Dec 31	Leeds U	A	38,468	2–0	Redknapp, Fowler
Jan 2	Norwich C	H	34,709	4–0	Scales, Fowler 2, Rush
Jan 14	Ipswich T	H	32,733	0–1	
Jan 24	Everton	H	39,505	0–0	
Feb 4	Nottingham F	A	25,418	1–1	Fowler
Feb 11	QPR	H	35,996	1–1	Scales
Feb 25	Sheffield W	A	31,964	2–1	Barnes, McManaman
Mar 4	Newcastle U	H	39,300	2–0	Fowler, Rush
Mar 14	Coventry C	H	27,183	2–3	Molby (pen), Burrows (og)
Mar 19	Manchester U	H	38,906	2–0	Bruce (og), Redknapp
Mar 22	Tottenham H	A	31,988	0–0	
Apr 5	Southampton	H	29,881	3–1	Rush 2, Fowler (pen)
Apr 9	Leeds U	H	37,454	0–1	
Apr 12	Arsenal	A	38,036	1–0	Fowler
Apr 14	Manchester C	A	27,055	1–2	McManaman
Apr 17	Leicester C	H	36,012	2–0	Fowler, Rush
Apr 29	Norwich C	A	21,843	2–1	Harkness, Rush
May 2	Wimbledon	A	12,041	0–0	
May 6	Aston Villa	A	40,154	0–2	
May 10	West Ham U	A	22,446	0–3	
May 14	Blackburn R	H	40.014	2–1	Barnes, Redknapp

Final league position: 4th

FA CUP

Date	Team	Venue	Att	Score	Scorer
3rd Round					
Jan 7	Birmingham C	A	25,326	0–0	
Third Round replay (Liverpool won 2–0 on penalties)					
Jan 18	Birmingham C	H	36,275	1–1(aet)	Redknapp
Fourth Round					
Jan 28	Burnley	A	20,551	0–0	
Fourth Round replay					
Feb 7	Burnley	H	32,109	1–0	Barnes
Fifth Round					
Feb 19	Wimbledon	H	25,124	1–1	Fowler
Fifth Round replay					
Feb 28	Wimbledon	A	12,553	2–0	Barnes, Rush
Sixth Round					
Mar 11	Tottenham H	H	39,592	1–2	Fowler

COCA-COLA CUP

Date	Team	Venue	Att	Score	Scorer
2nd Round					
1st L Sep 21	Burnley	H	23,359	2–0	Scales, Fowler
2nd L Oct 5	Burnley	A	19,032	4–1	Redknapp 2, Fowler, Clough
3rd Round					
Oct 25	Stoke C	H	32,060	2–1	Rush 2
4th Round					
Nov 30	Blackburn R	A	30,115	3–1	Rush 3
5th Round					
Jan 11	Arsenal	H	35,026	1–0	Rush
Semi–final					
1st L Feb 15	Crystal Palace	H	25,480	1–0	Fowler
2nd L Mar 8	Crystal Palace	A	18,224	1–0	Fowler
Final (at Wembley)					
Apr 2	Bolton W	N	75,595	2–1	McManaman 2

PLAYER RECORDS

Name	App	(Sub)	L. Goals	Other Goals
James	42			
Fowler	42		25	2 FA Cup, 4 League Cup
McManaman	40		7	2 League Cup
Barnes	38		7	2 FA Cup
Ruddock	37		2	
Redknapp	36	5	3	1 FA Cup, 2 League Cup
Rush	36		12	1 FA Cup, 6 League Cup
Scales	35		2	1 League Cup
Babb	33	1		
R Jones	31			
Bjornebye	31			
Thomas	16	7		
Molby	12	2	2	
Harkness	8		1	
Walters	7	11		
Wright	5	1		
Kennedy	4	2		
Nicol	4			
Clough	3	7		1 League Cup
Matteo	2	5		
L Jones	0	1		

John Scales gets a foot in the way of Chris Sutton during a 1995 clash with Blackburn

Year-by-year statistics – season 1995–96

	FA PREMIER LEAGUE				
Date	**Team**	**Venue**	**Att**	**Score**	**Scorer**
Aug 19	Sheffield W	H	40,535	1–0	Collymore
Aug 21	Leeds U	A	35,852	0–1	
Aug 26	Tottenham H	A	31,254	3–1	Barnes 2, Fowler
Aug 30	QPR	H	37,548	1–0	Ruddock
Sep 9	Wimbledon	A	19,350	0–1	
Sep 16	Blackburn R	H	39,502	3–0	Redknapp, Fowler, Collymore
Sep 23	Bolton Wanderers	H	40,104	5–2	Fowler 4, Harkness
Oct 1	Manchester U	A	34,934	2–2	Fowler 2
Oct 7	Coventry C	H	39,079	0–0	
Oct 22	Southampton	A	15,245	3–1	McManaman 2, Redknapp
Oct 28	Manchester C	H	39,267	6–0	Rush 2, Redknapp, Fowler 2, Ruddock
Nov 4	Newcastle U	A	36,547	1–2	Rush
Nov 18	Everton	H	40,818	1–2	Fowler
Nov 22	West Ham U	A	24,324	0–0	
Nov 25	Middlesbrough	A	29,390	1–2	Ruddock
Dec 2	Southampton	H	38,007	1–1	Collymore
Dec 9	Bolton Wanderers	A	21,042	1–0	Collymore
Dec 17	Manchester U	H	40,546	2–0	Fowler 2
Dec 23	Arsenal	H	39,806	3–1	Fowler 3
Dec 30	Chelsea	A	31,137	2–2	McManaman 2
Jan 1	Nottingham F	H	39,206	4–2	Fowler 2, Collymore, Cooper (og)
Jan 13	Sheffield W	A	32,747	1–1	Rush
Jan 20	Leeds U	H	40,254	5–0	Ruddock 2, Fowler 2 (1 pen), Collymore
Jan 31	Aston Villa	A	39,332	2–0	Collymore, Fowler
Feb 3	Tottenham H	H	40,628	0–0	
Feb 11	QPR	A	18,405	2–1	Wright, Fowler
Feb 24	Blackburn R	A	30,895	3–2	Collymore 2, Thomas
Mar 3	Aston Villa	H	39,508	3–0	McManaman, Fowler 2
Mar 13	Wimbledon	H	34,063	2–2	McManaman, Collymore
Mar 16	Chelsea	H	40,820	2–0	Wright, Fowler
Mar 23	Nottingham F	A	29,058	0–1	
Apr 4	Newcastle U	H	40,702	4–3	Fowler 2, Collymore 2
Apr 6	Coventry C	A	23,127	0–1	
Apr 9	West Ham U	H	40,326	2–0	Collymore, Barnes
Apr 16	Everton	A	40,120	1–1	Fowler
Apr 27	Middlesbrough	H	40,782	1–0	Collymore
May 1	Arsenal	A	38,323	0–0	
May 5	Manchester C	A	31,436	2–2	Lomas (og), Rush

Final league position: 3rd

UEFA CUP

Date	Team	Venue	Att	Score	Scorer
1st Round					
1st L Sep 12	Spartak Vladikavkaz	A	43,000	2–1	Redknapp, McManaman
2nd L Sep 26	Spartak Vladikavkaz	H	35,042	0–0	
2nd Round					
1st L Oct 17	Brondby IF	A	37,648	0–0	
2nd L Oct 31	Brondby IF	H	35,878	0–1	

FA CUP

Date	Team	Venue	Att	Score	Scorer
3rd Round					
Jan 6	Rochdale	H	28,126	7–0	Fowler, Collymore 3, Valentine (og), Rush, McAteer
4th Round					
Feb 18	Shrewsbury T	A	7,752	4–0	Collymore, Walton (og), Fowler, McAteer
5th Round					
Feb 28	Charlton A	H	36,818	2–1	Fowler, Collymore
6th Round					
Mar 10	Leeds U	A	24,632	0–0	
6th Round replay					
Mar 20	Leeds U	H	30,812	3–0	McManaman 2, Fowler
Semi–final (at Old Trafford)					
Mar 31	Aston Villa	N	39,072	3–0	Fowler 2, McAteer
Final (at Wembley)					
May 11	Manchester U	N	79,007	0–1	

COCA-COLA CUP

Date	Team	Venue	Att	Score	Scorer
2nd Round					
1st L Sep 20	Sunderland	H	25,579	2–0	McManaman, Thomas
2nd L Oct 4	Sunderland	A	20,560	1–0	Fowler
3rd Round					
Oct 25	Manchester C	H	29,394	4–0	Scales, Fowler, Rush, Harkness
4th Round					
Nov 29	Newcastle U	H	40,077	0–1	

PLAYER RECORDS

Name	App	(Sub)	L. Goals	Other Goals
McManaman	38		6	2 FA Cup, 1 League Cup, 1 European goal
James	38			
Fowler	35	3	28	7 FA Cup goals, 1 League Cup
Barnes	35	3		
Jones	33			
Collymore	31	1	14	5 FA Cup
Wright	28		2	
Babb	28			
McAteer	27	2		3 FA Cup
Scales	27			1 League Cup
Harkness	23	1	1	1 League Cup
Ruddock	19	2	4	1 League Cup
Redknapp	18	5	3	1 League Cup, 1 European
Thomas	15	11	1	1 League Cup
Rush	6	14	5	1 FA Cup, 1 League Cup
Matteo	5			
Kennedy	2	2		
Bjornebye	2			
Clough	1	1		

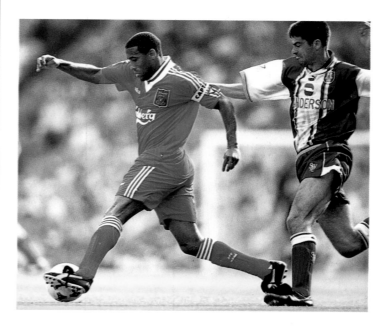

John Barnes in full stride during the 1–0 defeat of Sheffield Wednesday in August 1995

Year-by-year statistics – season 1996–97

				FA PREMIER LEAGUE	
Date	**Team**	**Venue**	**Att**	**Score**	**Scorer**
Aug 17	Middlesbrough	A	30,039	3–3	Bjornebye, Barnes, Fowler
Aug 19	Arsenal	H	38,103	2–0	McManaman 2
Aug 24	Sunderland	H	40,503	0–0	
Sep 4	Coventry C	A	23,021	1–0	Babb
Sep 7	Southampton	H	39,189	2–1	Collymore, McManaman
Sep 15	Leicester C	A	20,987	3–0	Berger 2, Thomas
Sep 21	Chelsea	H	40,739	5–1	Fowler, Berger 2, Myers(og), Barnes
Sep 29	West Ham U	A	25,064	2–1	Collymore, Thomas
Oct 12	Manchester U	A	55,128	0–1	
Oct 27	Derby C	H	39,515	2–1	Fowler 2
Nov 3	Blackburn R	A	29,598	0–3	
Nov 16	Leeds U	A	39,981	2–0	Ruddock, McManaman
Nov 20	Everton	H	40,751	1–1	Fowler
Nov 23	Wimbledon	H	39,027	1–1	Collymore
Dec 2	Tottenham H	A	32,899	2–0	Thomas, McManaman
Dec 7	Sheffield W	H	39,507	0–1	
Dec 14	Middlesbrough	H	39,491	5–1	Fowler 4, Bjornebye
Dec 17	Nottingham F	H	36,126	4–2	Collymore 2, Fowler, Lyttle (og)
Dec 23	Newcastle U	A	36,570	1–1	Fowler
Dec 26	Leicester C	H	40,786	1–1	Collymore
Dec 29	Southampton	A	15,222	1–0	Barnes
Jan 1	Chelsea	A	28,329	0–1	
Jan 11	West Ham U	H	40,102	0–0	
Jan 18	Aston Villa	H	40,489	3–0	Carragher, Collymore, Fowler
Feb 1	Derby C	A	18,102	1–0	Collymore
Feb19	Leeds U	H	38,957	4–0	Fowler, Collymore 2, Redknapp
Feb 22	Blackburn R	H	40,747	0–0	
Mar 2	Aston Villa	A	39,339	0–1	
Mar 10	Newcastle U	H	40,751	4–3	McManaman, Berger, Fowler 2
Mar 15	Nottingham F	A	29,181	1–1	Fowler
Mar 24	Arsenal	A	38,068	2–1	Collymore, McAteer
Apr 6	Coventry C	H	40,079	1–2	Fowler
Apr 13	Sunderland	A	21,938	2–1	Fowler, McManaman
Apr 16	Everton	A	40,177	1–1	Thomsen (og)
Apr 19	Manchester U	H	40,892	1–3	Barnes
May 3	Tottenham H	H	40,003	2–1	Collymore, Berger
May 6	Wimbledon	A	20,016	1–2	Owen
May 11	Sheffield W	A	38,943	1–1	Redknapp

Final League position: 4th

EUROPEAN CUP-WINNERS' CUP

Date	Team	Venue	Att	Score	Scorer
1st Round					
1st L Sep 12	MyPa–47	A	5,500	1–0	Bjornebye
2nd L Sep 26	MyPa–47	H	39,013	3–1	Berger, Collymore, Barnes
2nd Round					
1st L Oct 17	FC Sion	A	16,500	2–1	Fowler, Barnes
2nd L Oct 31	FC Sion	H	38,514	6–3	McManaman, Bjornebye, Barnes, Fowler 2, Berger
Quarter–final					
1st L Mar 6	Brann Bergen	A	12,700	1–1	Fowler
2nd L Mar 20	Brann Bergen	H	40,326	3–0	Fowler 2, Collymore
Semi–final					
1st L Apr 10	Paris S.G.	A	45,142	0–3	
2nd L Apr 24	Paris S.G.	H	38,894	2–0	Fowler, Wright

FA CUP

Date	Team	Venue	Att	Score	Scorer
3rd Round					
Jan 4	Burnley	H	33,252	1–0	Collymore
4th Round					
Jan 27	Chelsea	A	27,950	2–4	Fowler, Collymore

COCA-COLA CUP

Date	Team	Venue	Att	Score	Scorer
3rd Round					
Oct 23	Charlton A	A	15,000	1–1	Fowler
3rd Round replay					
Nov 13	Charlton A	H	20,714	4–1	Wright, Redknapp, Fowler 2
4th Round					
Nov 27	Arsenal	H	32,814	4–2	McManaman, Fowler 2, Berger
Quarter–final					
Jan 8	Middlesbrough	A	28,670	1–2	McManaman

PLAYER RECORDS

Name	App	(Sub)	L. Goals	Other Goals
Bjornebye	38		2	2 European
James	38			
McManaman	37		7	1 European, 2 League Cup
McAteer	36	1	1	
Barnes	34	1	4	3 European
Wright	33			1 European, 1 League Cup
Fowler	32		18	7 European, 1 FA Cup, 5 League Cup
Thomas	29	2	3	
Collymore	25	5	12	2 European, 2 FA Cup
Matteo	23	4		
Babb	21	1	1	
Redknapp	18	5	2	1 League Cup
Kvarme	16			
Ruddock	15	2	1	
Berger	13	10	6	2 European, 1 League Cup
Harkness	5	2		
Scales	3			
R Jones	2			
Carragher	1	1	1	
Owen	1	1	1	
Kennedy	0	5		
Thompson	0	2		
L Jones	0	2		

Jamie Redknapp and Southampton's Alan Nielsen tussle for possession in a 2–1 win for the Reds

Acknowledgements

The publishers would like to thank the following sources for their kind permission to reproduce the pictures in this book:

All Action/ Suzan Moore; Allsport UK Ltd./Shaun Botterill, Clive Brunskill, David Cannon, Mike Cooper, Mike Hewitt, Clive Mason, Mike Powell, Ben Radford, Dan Smith, Mark Thompson, Anton Want; Allsport Historical Collection/Hulton Getty; Associated Press; Colorsport/ Matthew Impey; Empics/ Steve Marriott, Steve Morton; Liverpool Daily Post and Echo; M.S.I.; Popperfoto/Reuters; PA News/ Phil Lewis; Professional Sport; Gordon Whiting.

Every effort has been made to acknowledge correctly and contact the source and/copyright holder of each picture, and Carlton Books Limited apologises for any unintentional errors or omissions which will be corrected in future editions of this book.